ORDINARY
HEROES

ORDINARY
HEROES

Teenage Adversity Inspires

Acts of Courage

James MacDicken

To order additional copies of this book, contact:
Xlibris Corporation
1-888-795-4274
www.Xlibris.com
Orders@Xlibris.com
43429

CONTENTS

DEDICATION

For all the times she has sacrificed, advised, and respectfully given of herself without any return expectations, I dedicate this book to my wife, Jan of 40 years.

INTRODUCTION

We are constantly exposed to negative role models that receive attention for hurting our society and ignoring basic morals. The media searches for stories that deal with human suffering and violence. Stories of mindless predators and helpless victims seem to increase public interest and fuel sales. Once in a while we will read a story about a young person who performed a heroic deed or act. But most of the time these do not sell and are relegated to the back pages of the paper or special interest stories on early morning television. In lieu of the most recently publicized actions of violence committed by young people across the nation, we need stories that demonstrate positive contributions on an everyday basis. These accounts need not necessarily be of a monumental level. They can be stories that have no sensational impact, but still demonstrate personal courage and integrity.

Throughout my tenure as a teacher in public education, I have been fortunate to share in the lives and worlds of thousands of young people. No matter what the background or experience, each one has a story to tell. However, there are a few that stand out above the rest. They have demonstrated tremendous strength and character in overcoming obstacles and meeting a challenge. Most of the time only a few people, if any, notice these subtle and quiet acts. Yet to those who take notice, they may be instrumental in bringing personal growth and change. Since my life has personally been so greatly enriched by these ordinary heroes, I would like to briefly share a few of their inspiring and quiet stories.

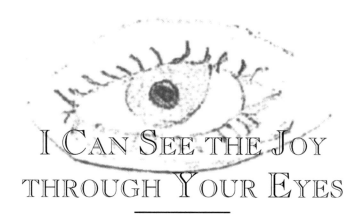

I Can See the Joy
through Your Eyes

All people need to feel important or at least receive some sort of notoriety. If a person is unable to find a social niche within a given group, her or she will withdraw, rebel, or leave that particular group. In public and private schools, there always seems to be an interplay or a conflict between the "in group" and the "counterculture." Others will play various roles in hopes of acceptance and some degree of status. Young people, like adults, seem to attain status in a number of ways. Wealth, talent, knowledge, appearance, and rebellion are some of the major means of attaining acceptance. However the particulars seem to vary according to the rules set down by a given social structure.

Students in a given school will inadvertently or intentionally establish unwritten rules for students to follow. If they do not follow these rules, they will rebel, withdraw, or change the structure. Kurt could easily be identified with the rebellious group. He was repeatedly kicked out of class, suspended from school, or served detention time. His clique or group would hang out across from the school smoking "duggars" and complaining. The group would repeatedly skip school, vandalize property, or harass the other students. In the past, groups of this nature received the normal amount of attention through their actions. They would intimidate, frighten, or repulse students. But either way, they received their desired status.

Sarcasm and vulgarity also reinforced the group's reputation. But a change was beginning to occur at our school. These types of people were losing their influence and power. Other students began to see the insecurity and emotional pain these "rebels" harbored. Students no longer were intimidated by these childish actions; in fact, the students began to pity these people. Consequently many influential leaders and athletes made an effort to rectify the problem by including all the students in school-related activities. Needless to say, most counterculture people refused. It was hard for them to abandon a social structure that had previously given them status and power. Even though they were befriended and included, their egos made it difficult to change. The "establishment" represented everything they had made mockery of and disdained. Even though Kurt had a few friends on athletic teams or involved in student government, he was still reluctant to swallow their sales pitch.

But Kurt was unique or different from the many who are associated with his group. He liked competitive sports despite having only average ability himself. Maybe it was the fear of failure or lack of discipline, but Kurt never turned out for sports in high school. And although he was intelligent and creative, he never became involved in other extracurricular activities, such as drama or music. This could also be attributed to his longtime association with the "counterculture." But I personally think that there is much more to it.

True, Kurt liked to be the center of attention. But there was much more to him than that. He had this genuine underlying concern for others. He was one of those people who were entertained and sincerely interested in activities and talents of other people. The more I got to know this young man, the more I realized how unique he was. I would watch him when he would talk to other students. As they spoke about their interests or achievement, his eyes would sparkle with enthusiasm. He even would generate more discussions with questions and congratulations.

Some of the athletes had made a special effort to ask Kurt to help advertise for upcoming events. He unselfishly agreed to advertise openly in casual conversations with friends and classmates. This also gave Kurt additional motivation to attend events himself. He started going to the boys and girls basketball games. He would scream and began to start chants to involve the fans. He would express genuine excitement and interest when recounting the games the following day. We had had good attendance before, but with the selling job Kurt gave, our attendance soared to near capacity for each event. Even most of his counterculture friends began to attend. Athletes from swimming and wrestling teams requested his support and enthusiasm. Soon those teams started to get a large following. Eventually, cheering and supporting all school events became the "in" thing.

It spilled over to the music and drama departments. Almost every concert and drama production was sold out. And of course, the first one to arrive was Kurt. It had become a social rule of expectation to support all activities. It grew to the point that over 85 percent of the student body was involved in sports or other activities. The participation and enthusiasm affected the overall spirit in school. It spilled over into the classroom. Grades and attendance soared. The enthusiasm and positive attitude had such a positive effect on doubters and ego-challenged students when it was reverberating through the entire school. The foundation was laid for a new tradition of involvement and enthusiasm. This mutual support and admiration became so reciprocal that the teams began giving the fans awards. An example of this unique interaction was when the girls' basketball team awarded the student body a trophy of appreciation as the most supportive fans in the state. All people who work in education should have at least one such experience.

Kurt was only one of the many who initiated this enthusiasm and school spirit. But he certainly was the most consistent, reliable, and unselfish in his support. The student body officers recognized his impact and rewarded him by starting a new tradition. At the last assembly of his junior year, Kurt was awarded with a plaque and title as Fan of the Year. He symbolized what a true fan and supporter of peers should be. His sincere joy for others was a model for all.

Kurt's senior year was filled with new and exciting challenges. But nobody could foresee the new set of hurdles that needed to be jumped. During the early spring of Kurt's senior year, some shocking news developed. He was diagnosed with a severe case of cancer. It seemed he might well be at the point of no return. Doctors felt that his cancer had spread so far that chemo and radiation therapies were almost pointless. The student body was in shock. Questions arose that seemed to cloud perspective. People were confused, frustrated, and looked for justice in an unjust situation. All we could do was hope that the lessons learned could now be applied to something far more significant.

It was now time for all of his friends to rally behind him. Hundreds of students made numerous visits to the hospital to show unified support for Kurt. There were a lot of prayers, tears, and pain spreading through the student body. For six weeks he fought an uphill battle to lick the cancer. Suddenly and almost with no warning the cancer turned. Within another two months the cancer was completely gone. Our number 1 fan had taught unselfish giving; and ironically, it was returned to him by the entire student body. Mutual support had been reciprocated, and the lessons learned left an impact on all of us.

There Is Tough and There Is Sally

Intense, feisty, competitive, and yet feminine and a true lady. All of these adjectives were accurate. She was the toughest and one of the most ethical student athletes I have ever had the privilege to teach or coach. She was respectful of all and intimidated by none. She was a lady who was a representation of liberation ahead of her time. Sally was and is truly a strong and tough young lady who always placed principle above selfish goals.

She had been a student of mine in two different classes. She was a person who injected sincere enthusiasm and curiosity to any discussion or subject. This intensity inspired others to reach a higher level of achievement and concentration. She demonstrated her knowledge and thorough understanding by consistently scoring in the top 5 percent of the class on tests and quizzes. And she would accept this success with a genuine indifference or even humility. She would never brag about herself and was quick to offer accolades to her peers. She would be insulted and even become indignant if she ever thought that she was given something that she had not earned or deserved. If a person ever wanted to feel the heat raise, all they would have to do is comment about her being just a girl or act in a condescending manner. Consequently, in any competitive situation, an opponent better have it strapped on or they were in for a whirlwind of a ride.

In class, she would become impatient if we ever wavered away from educational goals or subject matter. I recall a number of occasions when Sally would express anxiety if class were ever a little slow in getting started. These high expectations and personal demands were evident in all of the roles that she played. She also applied these intense goal-orientation characteristics as a three-sport athlete, cheerleader, and student body officer. It is not an understatement when I say that Sally could fire the kiln or move anybody to action.

It was my first year of coaching girls' basketball. I had accepted the position on a temporary basis as a favor to the athletic director. Our girls basketball program had struggled under different coaches in its first three years. However, I noted unexpected qualities during the first three days of practice. Most of these young ladies reflected the leadership qualities of Sally. They were competitive, tough, and to a fault-unselfish. There were a number of times that I would have to plead for them to shoot the ball and not overpass. The unselfish competitive attitude should not be questioned. The challenge, as a coach, was to convince these young ladies of their ability and potential.

The athletes worked hard to blend as a team and realize their dreams. However, we were cursed with a barrage of injuries. At one time, five out of our top six players were sidelined with severe ankle sprains. I began to question my training methods and myself. I even contacted a well-known and experienced college coach and asked if I was pushing them too hard or not giving them sufficient time to recover. After a few humorous and sarcastic remarks, she gave me full assurance that we had not offended the injury "mojo," and time would stabilize these skewed odds.

We continued to limp through the season with an even win-loss record. I still was impressed at how hard these gritting and tough athletes competed. Following Sally's lead, the intensity level even increased. This gave honor to the team, school, and basketball in general. These young ladies played the game the way it is supposed to be played. Fans began filling up the gym. This team would prove to serve as a role model for future groups at the school. They built a foundation in the program that left a legacy and a code of behavior. It amazed me how younger players whose teams had far better records would repeatedly refer to this team as an example to honor and follow. A tradition was established.

Sally had demonstrated this pride to a fault. On one occasion, we were playing a team who had been state champions two out of the last three years. They had thoroughly thrashed Sally and her crew the previous year. However, the "beating" did not dissuade these young ladies of the task ahead. We knew we could play with and even defeat this team. That confidence, coupled with the probability that the other team was fighting, the old complacent disease fueled our intensity level. We battled right down to the wire. But in the end, we suffered a bitter and disappointing three-point loss. Needless to say, the girls were discouraged.

The opposing coach was justifiably impressed with the improvement and effort of the team. He expressed admiration and respect by complimenting each of our team members. When he shook Sally's hand, an unexpected response occurred. She quickly pulled her hand away and exclaimed, "Don't patronize me." The coach was speechless and in shock as he walked away shaking his head in disbelief. Sally's competitive drive and respect for her fellow teammates surfaced as rude and classless behavior.

I quickly took Sally aside and told her in no uncertain terms that that kind of behavior could not be tolerated. It was a negative reflection on her and the team. My voice softened as I said, "Sally, as a leader, it is always necessary to demonstrate poise, dignity, and respect." She rebutted, "Coach, they were telling us that we played beyond expectations. What he really was telling me is that a losing effort is great for us." "I admire your team pride, but poor sportsmanship should never be displayed. Particularly by such a strong leader as yourself," I countered. "The coach was giving you a sincere compliment," I added. A moment of silence was quickly interrupted with a deep sigh and a confused expression. "Yeah, I guess I know that they were trying to demonstrate class and give us respect. But in the heat of the moment, I felt they were arrogant and looking down their noses at us," she said.

The situation had to be rectified. Her eyes narrowed, and her shoulders drooped when I informed her that it would be necessary for her to go apologize. She slowly got up and made her way over to the coach who was busy talking with a newspaper reporter. While shifting her weight from one foot to another, she patiently waited for a chance to speak with him. Finally the interview was completed, and he turned toward Sally. They respectfully exchanged words and shook hands. The coach then gave her a positive nod as she slowly made her way back. I never asked either of them what was said, but I am sure that the communication resulted in a positive feeling between them. It is my hope that pride and self-confidence had been tempered with class and demonstrated respect.

Sally's mental state, leadership skills, and tough physical play made her a prime candidate to take on the biggest challenges. Consequently, we would always have her guard the best player on the opposing team. It didn't matter if she was six feet two inches and powerful or five feet three inches and quick. She relished the challenge and was eager to overcome any obstacle presented. She was tenacious and rugged to say the least. Her dogged attitude, quick hands and feet, and sheer hustle would frustrate any opponent. If she did not get into foul trouble, she would repeatedly shut down their highest-scoring athlete. Needless to say, she was the catalyst for our team, and her example was critically important.

We were now coming to the midpoint of our league play. Despite the rash of injuries, we were playing well. One day I noticed that Sally was limping in warm-ups before practice. I knew that if she demonstrates pain, it must be excruciating. When questioned, she seemed a bit defensive. She said that she had had this pain in her shins for the past three weeks. "Once I get warmed up, the pain generally goes away," she said matter-of-factly. She must have done a great job of hiding the pain the past few practices and games. But that did not surprise me.

In the next few days, the limp became more noticeable. When I saw her dragging her foot, I told her that she had to get the leg checked. She looked away and ignored my words. I waited for a few seconds. She finally looked at me and nodded. "No nods, I need a promise," I said. Reluctantly, she agreed. The next day at practice, she informed me that she had the leg checked, and the doctor had told her that it was "just" shin splints. "The doctor said that if I could stand the pain, I can continue to play," she happily stated. And as anyone who knew her expected, she gutted out the rest of the season. It seemed as if she had constructed a new slogan: "The more it hurts, the harder I play."

As mentioned earlier, Sally was one of the most sincere and honest student-athletes I have ever known. As far as I know, she only sacrificed that principle once. The Monday following our last game, she came to school on crutches. After class, she sheepishly hobbled up to my desk and said, "Coach, I owe you an apology." What I told you was only partially true. I do have shin splints. But I also have a stress fracture," she muttered. Apparently, when she first went to the doctor, he had told her to take some pills for swelling, ice the injury, and come back the next day for a cast. It seems that she had also buffaloed her father. She had both of us convinced that what she had said was completely accurate. I know that he, too, must have had mixed feelings.

Sally and her father went in to see the doctor together after the season was over. When I spoke with him at the awards night, he told me that the doctor had said that it seemed almost impossible for her to play through such excruciating pain. Apparently, Sally was so consumed about her role and responsibility to the team that she was able to block the pain.

When I had first heard of the seriousness of the injury, I was outwardly angry and expressed disgust. Inwardly, I could not help but admire this young lady for her courage, toughness, selfless attitude, and overall maintenance of class and poise.

She is so talented, competitive, and goal oriented that I can picture her today in a wide variety of successful life roles and occupations. She will demand honesty and mutual respect from fellow "team members," competitors, and herself. And I know that she is playing the "game" with the same intensity and heart that she exhibited on the basketball court and in the classroom.

Does Your View Put Limits on Me?

When Howard came into my room the third week of school, I knew a favor or special request was on his personal agenda. Howard knew that his favorite patsies (teachers) were available for his special duties or experiments. Howard was a stern and demanding counselor. Yet this strong and unyielding personality did a futile job of covering up a heart that felt deeply for all young people. He also had a sincere appreciation for diverse individuals who exhibited unique or different intellectual and personal characteristics.

On one particular day, Howard was unusually pleasant and cordial. I knew that his request was out of the ordinary. He quietly asked permission to speak with me. He wanted to know if I would allow a severely handicapped individual in my paced or C-track class. He assured me that if this young man, whose cerebral palsy limited his ability to communicate and understand, was too heavy a burden I could have him withdrawn and returned to his previous contained classroom. We agreed on a three-week trial run.

Gary had severe speech and motor skill limitations. For the first two weeks, the students in the class who grew up with Gary had to translate his written or spoken word. I did note that Gary seemed to possess excellent concentration and listening skills.

Obviously, Gary would take a long time to complete a written assignment or test. He may have to take a class assignment or quiz home. He assured me that quizzes or tests would be completed without notes. He was so sincere and perceptive that I never challenged his honesty. On a number of occasions, Gary chose to finish an exam before or after school.

After three weeks, Howard and I briefly met regarding the adjustment and progress of Gary. I informed Howard that I wanted more time to work with and evaluate him. During the next two or three weeks, he became more comfortable and started answering questions and injecting ideas. Soon I realized that not only did he possess a massive amount of knowledge, Gary could encode and apply very quickly. It got to the point where he would answer questions so quickly, that much of the Socratic or solving process was eliminated. Since the whole class could now understand him, inquiring and solving problems themselves was replaced by the "ask Gary" method.

I entered Howard's office to discuss Gary's progress. When I informed him that I wanted to move Gary, Howard began to give me that sympathetic and I understand nod. Before I could finish, Howard stated that he suspected that the experiment with Gary might very well fail. "No, no," I replied. I want him moved to my B or medium-paced class." Howard raised his eyebrows in disbelief. "I do not want to move him back to the C track," he said. I assured him that that would never happen. Much to Howard's and my surprise, it quickly became evident that the B level of class was also far below his capabilities. Gary was moved to my A or accelerated class. This would be a shocking revelation to all educators who have a tendency to restrict or overprotect handicapped individuals. A young man had gone from a restricted self-contained class to a mainstreamed 4 point student in one short year.

It was rewarding to observe Gary overcome academic obstacles and meet and exceed expectations. It also was a true inspiration to watch him socially interact with peers on a friendly and mutually respectful basis. Gary and his friends had a unique, yet normal, relationship. Friends did not feel obligated to help or coddle Gary. They respected him as their equal. They all knew that each person had extraordinary talents and also personal limitations. Gary's peers were the most unselfish, objective, and giving males I have encountered in over thirty years of education. I am sure that their lives were impacted, and each grew in depth as a person because of their association with Gary. Likewise, I think that his strong and unselfish qualities were strengthened from his association with these quality people.

One morning, Gary and his friends were sitting at a resource center table. It was before school, and all at the table were hysterically laughing and joking. It seems that they had all been out the night before riding go-carts. Gary was taking a sharp turn when his cart suddenly veered off the track and crashed into a group of bushes. His friends rushed toward the shrieks coming from the bush. When they got to the bush, where the noise was coming, they saw two feet sticking out and swaying back and forth. They quickly grabbed the feet and pulled out a gasping Gary. His concerned friends were relieved to know that the shortage of breath came from his laughing. It probably was a typical day for Gary and his friends.

When the bell rang, all of his friends got up to go to class. Gary asked one of them to take his walker to the next floor. The friend snatched the walker and sarcastically agreed only if he would promise to work on his driving skills. I guess this was just another day in the life of an upbeat and positive person.

One Saturday morning there was a quiet knock on the door. When I opened the door, I was shocked to see Gary teetering on his three-wheel bike. I invited him in for what turned out to be a pleasant hour of conversation and jokes. After Gary turned down an invitation to lunch, he asked me if I knew where Mrs. Jungleville lived. The following is the short conversation that followed. "Sure, Gary, she lives at the top of Rivers Crest. Why do you ask?" I said. "I would like to visit her today also," he answered. "Gary, that is a three-to-four-mile ride that is a steep climb that goes straight up hill," I said. "I ride my two-wheel bike all the time, and that hill is next to impossible to traverse. Obviously, a three-wheel bike has much more drag and would be far more difficult," I added. "Yeah, I know, but the challenge would be fun, and besides, it is my goal to visit both of you today," he said. I realized that it was hopeless to try to dissuade Gary from his endeavor. As I watched him riding his bulky bike off in the distance, I could not help but wonder why a person with so many obstacles could exhibit and practice such unassuming courage. As expected, he completed his ride and had a wonderful visit with Mrs. Jungleville.

After being with Gary, a person would probably forget he was limited. He always had a way of making other people feel at ease. I have no idea how many individuals Gary has affected or touched in his life. Because he never complained, indulged in self-pity, put limitations on himself, or wore his hardships as a badge, I am sure he has left his legacy for many to note and take inspiration from. I do not know where Gary is today. The last I heard was that after completing high school in three years, receiving a bachelor of arts degree in two and a half years and a masters in a year, he was doing research for a large chemical corporation. And the one thing I am certain about is that he will continue having a curious zest for life and unselfishly give of himself to enrich the lives of others.

IT IS MY FAULT

I had just accepted a position as head football coach at a different school. The program had been "struggling" the past number of years. Not only had they won just one league game in the last four years, but also the number of players had dwindled to practically nothing. They had been forced to eliminate the junior varsity program, and the varsity had only thirteen players left.

Whenever a new person enters a sinking program, there seems to be a sense of hope and anticipation. Even though there were only about fifteen prospective players that attended the first meeting, there seemed to be individuals sincere and dedicated to the point that a reconstruction was possible. Andrew had the typical "buffoonery" associated with people who had high hopes yet little success and confidence. I had hoped that he would walk the walk rather than continue to brag and talk about his talents. I met with Andrew and the other prospective athletes on an individual basis. I could tell by his presence and movement that he had potential to be a leading athlete. Other people looked up to him despite his insecurities. It was essential to the program to have him lead in a positive and unselfish manner.

We needed to increase the numbers. We held meetings, wrote letters, visited homes, and had special and individual workouts. My assistant coaches were so important in helping to bring in over one hundred prospective athletes for our first doubles practice. It seemed that the program had gotten off the ground, and the new era was under way. The players were enthusiastic and eager to meet new challenges. Spirit, hard work, and unselfish attitudes were the norm at camp and in the early season. The players were primed and anxious for the first ball game. The enthusiasm only dropped slightly after losing a heartbreaker to a formidable foe the second game of the season. The winning touchdown pass had just barely been tipped away with a few seconds remaining on the clock.

However, after the third game (first league game) of the season, our earlier enthusiasm was being threatened and challenged. After being ahead by two touchdowns at halftime, we had managed to lose a one-point game. To make matters worse, two touchdowns had been called back because of penalties in the last four minutes of the game. All the sacrifice, teamwork, and high hopes were being challenged; and the very foundation of our team was shaken.

When I came to school Monday morning, I could see that Andrew and Kelly were depressed and frustrated. I called both men into my office before school started. I explained that they were the leaders of the team, and much of our success depended on how they responded to adversity. "Coach, nothing has really changed from the past. We are tougher and more competitive, but we are still losing," Andrew exclaimed. I repeated a philosophy of coaching that I have always stressed and believed. "Performance cannot truly be measured by wins and losses," I stated. "Positive or negative circumstances can lead to success or failure on the scoreboard. We need to evaluate our performance by our effort, competitive drive, desire to succeed, and willingness to accept responsibility,"

I added. "But, Coach, nobody outside of our team understands this," Kelly replied. "You are absolutely right, and maybe that is what makes the effort so special. Only you and your teammates should be the ones to address and feel that genuine bond of effort," I said. I told them that they must rise above embarrassment, selfishness, and irresponsible behavior. They had to demonstrate leadership by setting an example that emphasized mental toughness. "If you exhibit these qualities, we as coaches cannot help but always be in your corner," I stated.

This was a very difficult role for these young men to play. Their uncertain feelings seemed to be reinforced by fellow classmates who relished in their frustration and failure. Later, as I was walking down the hall during lunch, I observed Andrew talking emphatically to a group of skeptics and "frontrunners." He had his back to me, and I believe he was unaware of my presence. "This is my team, and I will support them no matter what happens. My teammates have the guts to put themselves on the line despite all of you people who believe we are losers. Who is a loser, the one who tries and makes an effort or the one who sits in the stands and complains?" he said. I quickly turned the corner and walked away. This young man was making a private and personal statement. I felt an overwhelming sense of pride and confidence in the team and its leaders.

The next week we were to face the undefeated, number 1 team in the league. We played the game in front of two hundred fans without fanfare or game hype. Many in the stands were anxious to watch the slaughter. They knew that we were overwhelming underdogs. The game was filled with tough, defensive play. We still were not over the hump. Players wanted to excuse themselves and point fingers. All of a sudden the game took a turn for the worse. Andrew fumbled a pitch that was recovered by our opponents on our own thirty-four-yard line. It only took seven plays for them to score. The hopes were shattered. All of a sudden, a single voice rose above the frustrated and quiet moans. "We will get it back; that score was my fault," Andrew blurted. The bench was silent for a good five seconds as the players looked at each other in astonishment. Their leader was not pointing fingers. He had taken the responsibility upon himself. It was as if Andrew had given us a jump-start. With the spirit and intensity regained, the team reunited, and momentum was beginning to swing in our favor. We battled to a standstill the rest of the first half.

On the opening kickoff of the second half, Kelly took the ball and followed his blockers for an eighty-six-yard kickoff return. We missed the extra point that would have tied the game, but there seemed to be an atmosphere of confidence. The fans were treated to a game of gang tackling and tough play. Early in the fourth quarter, Andrew took a pitch and romped thirty yards for a touchdown. He then ran in the extra point to give us a 14-7 lead. However, championship teams do not let adversity force them to quit. With seconds left in the game, their all-state running back broke loose for a twenty-three-yard touchdown run. When they lined up for the extra point, I could hear Andrew leading a cheer. "You gotta believe," they were yelling. When the center snap was low and the holder fumbled the placement, the kick was delayed and blocked. After congratulating the opponents, the team celebrated as if they had won a championship. Normally such celebration should be delayed until the completion of a season, but these young men had endured such tribulations that they deserved to relish in the group effort and success. It was apparent that this game acted as a springboard to a fulfilling season.

Prior to a key game to be played against a team that had handled our team by forty or fifty points the previous two seasons, Andrew was forced to come late to practice because of a school field trip. Our rule stated that if a person had an excused absence or tardy and fulfilled the running requirements, they were eligible to play but not as a "starter." One of the other players had earlier come to me and pleaded the case of Andrew. He stated that the tardiness was something that could not be avoided, and Andrew should be allowed to start. He also felt that Andrew would be frustrated because of this unavoidable situation. Even though I already had heard of the field trip, I thanked him and stated that rules could not be altered because of diverse circumstances. "Andrew is going to be upset about this," he stated. I just smiled and nodded.

It was a pregame practice as we put the final touches on our game plan. Andrew had missed about thirty minutes of practice time that day. I went up to talk with Andrew after he completed his sprints for being late. As we were walking off the field after practice, I said matter-of-factly, "You know that you will not start in tomorrow's game." He looked me straight in the eyes and said, "I know the rules, and of course I would not expect to start. That would be insulting to me and my team." It was a short and respectful exchange of statements. He passed it by quickly, and we began to discuss the game plan. I admired his businesslike approach and desire to focus on the task at hand.

This team went on to win many games. They made a serious run at the playoffs and were rewarded the title of Team of the Year for the state, by a local radio station. The reward was accepted with honor and pride. But this team did not need the award. The hard work, honesty and unselfishness, and growth were their own rewards.

DIPLOMACY OPENED
BY INTEGRITY

She came from an upper-class family. Her parents were constructively involved in all aspects of her athletic career. They were always willing to play any role necessary to help facilitate success for all the members of the team. It is so easy for parents, who have financial means, to spoil or indulge their children. However, there seemed to always be a sense of objectivity about her and the feelings for her fellow team members. While always being there to support Candy, her parents were more concerned about giving her a sense of balance and worth.

We noted her natural talent right from the start. She picked up skills very quickly. She would work hard to refine and improve these skills. But there was so much more to Candy as an athlete. She was gregarious and enthusiastic on and off the basketball court. Her enthusiasm on the court was tempered with concentration that drove her competitive nature to reach the highest of personal and team goals. She would constructively challenge her teammates to perform at a high level, and then pat them on the back or ease the tension with a wry smile. When pressure would increase, she could inject a joke or a laugh to break the tensions, but not distract from overall goals. If players became sloppy or indifferent, she would verbally challenge team members to increase concentration or effort. It was remarkable how she could inject the proper emotion through words or gestures to attain or maintain balance.

She was very much aware of the needs of the individual and the team. If the team began floundering, she would meet the challenge. Numerous times in her career she would rescue our team from despair by playing any role necessary to facilitate success. If we needed to shut down an opponent, facilitate the fast break or score thirty points, she would unselfishly play the missing role. Candy was a coach's dream: unselfish, talented, and dedicated. Those qualities helped her realize numerous accolades, awards, and opportunities. She was a first-team all-state player in both volleyball and basketball. She was offered numerous opportunities at the collegiate level in both sports. After much deliberation, she decided to play basketball at a small Division I school. She chose this particular university because of certain intangibles. First of all, she had deep respect for the coaching staff. They demonstrated a primary concern for the student-athlete as a whole. They spent most of the visitation time discussing educational opportunities, team unity, and the future of each member. These qualities are so rare for coaches who face expectations and demands from fans and alumni that are primarily concerned with wins and scoreboards. She also sensed a university dedicated to the education of all students. Thirdly, she chose a school that was close enough to home to allow her family to share in her experiences. She was now set to pursue a career as a student athlete at the Division I level.

Candy was never a person to rest on her laurels. She had achieved much in her high school career. Yet, like so many great athletes, she wanted to improve her skills and level of play. She worked very hard during the spring and summer before her first year in college. She practiced with diligence and purpose all summer in preparation for her freshman year. I remember the day before she left how excited, determined, and a bit uncertain she was. We knew that Candy loved these feelings. Yet she loved team play and the game of basketball even more. She was a true fan of the game and had always participated for the right reasons.

How she dealt with her freshman year in college was a true measurement of her quality as a balanced and unselfish person. When she arrived on campus, she heard a rumor that was depressing and shocking. Her coach and his staff may be leaving for another school. That night the coach brought the team members in to confirm the rumor. He assured them that the university was committed to hiring the best coach for the upcoming season. He emphasized the importance of sticking together. He then assured the players that the decision was difficult to make, and that he would follow their season and careers with interest. Candy was crushed. She had been so careful to choose a program that had coaches she admired and respected. These coaches were now gone and the ground rules changed. Despite being disappointed and frustrated, she felt obligated to stick by her commitment.

The new coach arrived shortly after the discouraging news. The team found it difficult to bond and form a sense of unity. Although individual members worked hard to create a team with a strong and unique personality, some of the players decided to leave. Candy refused to jump ship and continued to work hard to improve to help bring about team success.

The new coach brought in a different style of play. The pressing and fast-breaking team that Candy thrived on in high school and was being built at the university was being replaced by a deliberate and slow-paced offense. Even though the team struggled, it did show signs of improvement. The coach impressed upon the players that a change and success would take time. He also encouraged the team to stick together and not abandon the ship. Candy's best friend and roommate chose to leave after the season was done. The parting from the team created hard and bitter feelings.

Candy was frustrated and knew that this style of play would limit her unique abilities as a player. She found no fault with the new coach and understood why the change was being made. Yet her skills and experience seemed to be going to waste. She was torn between loyalty and personal achievement.

She made a concerted effort to speak with the coach numerous times about where he saw the team going in the future. She knew that changing to another school could result in her loss of scholarship and sitting out a full year. But Candy was always a person of high integrity and ethics. She understood the need for loyalty. Yet she wanted to play where she would best help a team and realize her potential. So she requested a meeting with the coach. During the meeting, she expressed her concern for the direction of the team. Although she genuinely understood his motives in changing the style of play to match the skills of many of his players, she felt it could also restrict or inhibit her style.

This was a gamble because Candy did not want to burn a bridge and keep the avenues of communication open with the coach. What resulted was a solid communication between player and coach. The coach and Candy respectfully discussed various concerns and suggested solutions. Because of this mutual respect, they decided that it was okay for Candy to search for other options. After being accepted to play at a larger and more prestigious school with full scholarship, she decided to meet with the coach again. She expressed her dilemma. The coach responded by supporting her and helping her with the NCAA. She was able to transfer with good conscience and the full support of her coach. Today, they are true friends and cheer for each other's accomplishments. The responsibility and maturity that Candy demonstrated help make her unique and a positive role model. There is no doubt that this poised and respectful young lady will have an influence on others facing divided options. Her success on and off the court is a testimony to how respect, maturity, and understanding bring an attitude of cooperation and mutual growth.

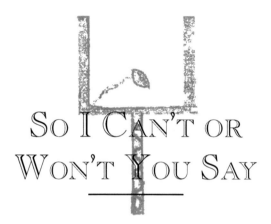

So I Can't or Won't You Say

Teenagers are not much different than adults when it comes to the development of the ego and status. All people strive for recognition, and the need for attention does not dissipate with age. Teenagers may not be as sophisticated or phony in their means of gaining status. But the need for positive reinforcement may be greater because of their developing egos.

If we as educators would take time to help fill the void created by feelings of inadequacy, we might be more successful in helping students realize their academic and personal potential. Sometimes we may find it difficult to help others when we are experiencing personal frustrations and challenges. And, oftentimes, when we do extend ourselves, it is a personal gamble and open to frustration. And if we have a tendency to wear our feelings on our shirtsleeves, we may not be ready for the obstacles encountered.

Tristan was a youngster who constantly needed assurance and reinforcement. He wanted to realize his dream of becoming an impact basketball player. He would brag or verbally challenge any person who would listen. He portrayed himself as a legend in his own mind. Despite some of this necessary verbal garbage, it never seemed to supersede his willingness to play any role to help facilitate team goals. For example, he would set solid screens, work hard on the boards, and play tough and relentless defense. These qualities were noted and praised by coaches. However, teammates and peers may only mouth their appreciation for the unsung hero. Points created by spectacular moves or a soft, shooting touch were more effective in giving status necessary to boost the self-image. In these areas, Tristan did not measure up to his personal expectations or performances by his teammates.

Nevertheless, Tristan continued to work hard to hone and develop his offensive skills. As a matter of fact, he decided to forgo his sophomore year of football and concentrate on basketball. He made the junior varsity as a sophomore. Even though he did not crack the starting lineup, he received plenty of playing time as the sixth or seventh man. However, Tristan was aware of the fact that seven or eight sophomores were ahead of him. Some were playing full-time varsity. He knew that he was faced with a very steep challenge if he were to realize his goals.

He went out for track in hopes of improving his agility and speed. Minimal accomplishments in track only offered dim hope for future athletic achievement. Yet he remained strong in his hopes of realizing his dream.

As a junior, disappointment and frustration smothered his constant bragging and challenges. He had "matured" to the point that he understood his personal barriers and physical limitations. His grades began to reflect a feeling of failure and hopelessness. This downward spiral was depressing to watch. Apparently we had failed as coaches to help strengthen and stabilize this young man's self-image.

Tristan would make one more attempt at creating a social niche for himself. Unfortunately, his decision came very late. We had completed camp and were in our first week of daily doubles when he approached me after practice. "Coach, is there any way I would still be able to turn out for football?" he asked sheepishly. Normally, a request of this nature by a junior would go on deaf ears. But here was a young man who, in his own eyes, had met frustration and failure. He needed to belong and have a sense of worth and purpose. "I'll tell you what, Tristan, I will let you turn out and play junior varsity football this year. However, you must run three hundred laps for missed practices before you can play in a game," I replied. Since the JV coach had requested that he have a chance to play, and we knew of some extenuating circumstances, I felt that this was a fair compromise. Doubt was evident in his face as he reluctantly agreed and quietly shuffled toward the door. His response was not what I had expected or hoped for.

I told Tristan that the manager would count every lap that he ran. The next day he began to run his laps after practice. After running sixty laps in two days, he quickly met a wall of despair. Toward the end of the practice, he informed the JV coach that he was going to quit. What followed was embarrassing to our entire program and athletics in general. Apparently, as Tristan walked off the JV practice field, the coaches and team members began to "sing" a song with a message of good-bye, loser. I was ashamed of the actions of all involved, and as the head coach, I had to accept the responsibility.

The next day the administration received a call from Tristan's irate mother. I heard that the administration was about to call the JV coach in on this disturbing matter.

However, I caught wind of the requested action. After discussing the matter with the administration, I told them that I would handle the problem, and there would be no further instances of this nature. I called the mother, and we talked for over thirty minutes. I requested an opportunity to counsel Tristan over the next few months. It was obvious that this event would be very difficult for Tristan to live down, and he would need extra help and support. Peers can be so tough on a young man after such an event. Over the next few weeks, we spoke often about his future and what means or actions may be necessary to meet his goals.

One morning he came to speak with me. Most of the times, our discussions were brief and generic in nature. This time Tristan had a mission. "Coach, I am going to tackle the problem in the classroom and become a very solid student," he stated with assurance. "I need to take care of my education first," he added. These statements did not have the usual doubt or baloney that, oftentimes, characterized some of his statements. These statements had a ring of sincerity and honest effort. There seemed to be a new determined attitude and perspective that could be identified in his eyes and voice.

Tristan lived up to and exceeded his promise. He diligently tackled his academic challenges and temporary obstacles. He received numerous academic honors for growth and achievement and eventually made the honor roll. He began to carry himself differently. He began to walk with his head up and spoke with a quiet and genuine confidence. The defensive words and gestures began to dissipate. He had become comfortable with himself and the direction in which he was headed.

This new confidence began to spill into other areas of Tristan's life. In late spring, he informed me that he wanted to turn out for football the following year. "I know that people think I am a loser and quitter, but I promise that will not happen," he emphatically said. His newly acquired self-discipline and motivation he had discovered through academic endeavors acted as a guide or springboard for athletics. He began by working hard all summer in the weight room. Many times he was the first to arrive and the last to leave the weight room. He also was the first to show up for camp in August. As for practice, he usually arrived early for our meetings and was the last to leave practice. At first his teammates were skeptical about his commitment to the team. However, after several days of noting dogged determination, they began to appreciate the change.

Physically he was not imposing. At six feet and 160 lbs., he was an unlikely outside linebacker. However, his technique was solid, and he played with such heart and determination. His demeanor had undergone a drastic change. He was humble and now let his actions do the talking. He would speak out strongly to compliment or support his teammates. He played extremely well and efficiently on both sides of the ball. I will never forget his juggling catch that pulled out our first major upset of the season. Numerous times he made outstanding offensive or defensive plays that were key to team success on the field. At the end of the season, he was chosen Most Inspirational Player by his teammates. He was also rewarded by being chosen as an Honorable Mention All-League Linebacker. There was no doubt that he would have been chosen first team in growth and resilience if such an award was offered.

But even more memorable, was his accomplishments as a student and how they aided in the development of a stronger and wiser personality. This young man had overcome numerous inner obstacles that oftentimes would bury weaker people. Just recently, I heard Tristan being interviewed on TV about priorities, education, and his fond memories of high school. His effort and resilience should be a beacon of inspiration to other students who have trouble finding a sense of worth or purpose. He truly was a young man who learned to abandon his excuses and defense mechanisms to focus on his means and goals that allowed him to reach a higher degree of satisfaction and self-worth.

Don't Undersell Me,
I Will Finish

Within the first fifteen minutes of basketball practice, I knew that this group was special. Among these freshmen, there were very distinctive personalities to say the least. They were mischievous, playful, and energetic. They loved to tease or harass each other. Many times we would have to stop practice to run lines for "punishment." But a coach could not help but have a feeling of closeness to each team member. They had a true zest for life and a genuine love for the game.

This group was not big, fast, or overly skilled. They had solid talent and played with great intensity. There were numerous intangibles that allowed this group to dominate larger and faster opponents. But one thing for certain, they always had fun and played with incredible heart.

One of the sparks on this team was Norven. He could verbalize cheap shots and offer inside jokes as well as anybody. His quick wit and sarcastic humor laid a solid foundation for a strongly unified and close group of athletes. A secondary factor was Norven had almost no use of one side of his body. He ran with a noticeable limp, and one withered arm was used solely for support.

He made the freshman team because of his heart and superior passing and dribbling skills. But his unwavering effort and intense hustle was a motivation to all of his fellow team members. He understood all aspects of the game and could lead verbally and by example.

When participating in open gym on Saturdays, he would surprise opponents with his superior moves and passing skills. The wry smiles and effortless body movements of challenged opponents quickly faded, and dogged determination would take over. He very quickly earned respect not because of his limitation, but because of his ability and intensity. Norven would do everything to hide his limitation because of his inner pride and disdain for pity and condescending attitudes. Although never wanting notice of his limitation, if a tease was directed toward him, he would not fire back defensively but would respond with wit that could "affectionately" sting.

Norven also participated in tennis. As one might conclude, he was skilled and a very tough competitor.

As a sophomore, he decided to turn out for football. Now, Norven was a respectful and cooperative player. Any humor was well timed and appropriate. He would play a role or do anything requested of him by a coach. His example of hard work and tireless effort was inspirational to fellow teammates. It became very difficult for other athletes to justify loafing or searching for excuses. Hard work and personal high expectations became the norm. Constructive criticism by coaches were openly accepted and looked upon as a positive challenge. Norven had laid the groundwork for all athletes to open themselves to challenges and a desire to put no limits on the individual or the team.

On one occasion we were in our second week of practice and involved in a tough series of exercises. We had told the players to finish off the exercise period by doing forty push-ups on their own. After seeing many players exhausted and struggling to complete the activity, I quietly leaned over to Norven and said, "You may finish these after practice." That was a mistake that was not intended. He gave me a cold stare and said through gritted teeth, "I will finish them now." This was not a statement of defiance, but strongly expressed out of pride and competitive drive. Normally, verbalizations of such manner cannot be tolerated. But as I turned and walked away, I was a bit embarrassed but felt an overwhelming sense of pride and admiration. Those few words have been an inspiration to me ever since. "Handicaps" are merely temporary obstacles to overcome so that others can vicariously grow and develop personal strength.

Norven made First Team All-League as a defensive back his senior year. I oftentimes picture that hand flashing in front of a receiver to knock down or intercept the ball. But moreover, I recall a man of courage, pride, humor, and unselfishness who never wore his limitations as an excuse or symbol for causes, but walked tall with pride and courage. Thank you for your unassuming courage and "cool" demeanor.

It's Time to Grow Up and Take Care of Your House

Young people, are all too often, attracted by negative role models. We, as a society, seem to reinforce negative behavior constantly through the media. People express disgust at all of these violent, vulgar, and disrespectful behaviors while giving attention and providing the very feedback and reinforcement the negative role models are looking for. It seems that any effort we make to discredit negative role models ends up reinforcing those personality characteristics being negatively portrayed.

Oftentimes, if a high school student were to vandalize his school, take drugs, skip school, or participate in a fight, he will not only receive attention from peers and school staff, but the act itself gives a sense of intrigue or power through rebellion. We are disgusted, appalled, or even frightened by such behavior. What we fail to understand or ignore is that these responses are exactly what the role model is striving to achieve.

Positive behavior can be labeled as "corny," old-fashioned, or "dweeby." Students who are honest, positive, or enthusiastic can be teased or ridiculed. We preach honesty, respect, hard work, and high morals.

Yet a young person who exemplifies these traits is ignored or laughed at by peers and society in general. These double messages confuse and make skeptics out of many of our youth. We even use clichés such as "grow up too soon," "experience the real world," or "live dangerously" to label negative behavior. It is obvious that these negative clichés are powerfully magnetic. If we used such terms as *childish*, *immature*, or *weak*, negative behavior would be less attractive to young people. Likewise, if we used words as *mature*, *strong*, or *influential*, we would have a better chance of reinforcing positive behavior.

Trying to be a role model who exemplifies courage and strength is a very a difficult task for a high school student to undertake. Dick decided to run for a student body office on a positive and straight ticket. His campaign speech did not include dirty jokes, slang, threats, or negative statements. It centered on positive goals and a means to attain them. Dick was liked and respected by his peers. He was not the negative "cool" that usually spells success in so many high schools. His initial failure in political endeavors had not dissuaded him from high aspirations.

It was refreshing to see that Dick was elected student body vice president in a runoff. His success was directly correlated with his personality. For instance, Dick always had the welfare of the school and other students at heart. He was willing to play any role that would help facilitate group success. He was gregarious and open to and with all social groups and cliques. He was willing to become unselfishly involved in other people's worlds. Whenever he conversed with other students, his body language demonstrated sincere interest in the person and the topic. He bridged the gap of cliques, personality differences, and biases. The open and nonjudgmental attitude of Dick could be noted almost every day in his selfless interaction with students and faculty.

One example of this open attitude occurred when a new student, Sam, enrolled one Monday morning. He was timid, shy, and uncertain. He spoke with a limited and uneducated vocabulary and demonstrated little flair or personality in his verbal and facial expressions. He was scared, insecure, and appeared defensive and bitter. He certainly did not present himself in an endearing manner to any classmates.

Immediately after class on Wednesday, Dick went up to this young man and said, "Hey, meet me for lunch, OK." Sam was a bit taken aback by the invitation but agreed with some reservation. For the next number of weeks, Sam ate lunch with Dick and his friends. Slowly Sam began to emerge from his shell. His grades improved, and his interest in school grew.

On Back to School Night, his mother came to me to express great appreciation for the students of our class. She particularly pointed out the efforts offered by Dick. She said that her son had always hated school and never had reached past minimum requirements. But he seemed to be a changed person with a new enthusiasm and perspective. I guess it was just a common practice for Dick to go out of his way to include people in activities and socializing.

Dick's awareness of the needs and inadequacies of others led him to work with and appreciate all people. His attitude was both influential and infectious. This open and friendly approach became the norm of behavior at the school. Needless to say, this was a school where people found their niche and wanted to stay.

Another example of Dick's leadership occurred one day during lunch. Some of the students, apparently, were in an edgy and devious mood. They decided to start a food fight in the cafeteria. After the barrage began, Dick quickly jumped up on top of the table. At the top of his voice, he yelled, "If you must play these childish games, do it at home and not in our school!" The fight stopped immediately, and the students sat down and continued their lunch. Because Dick was strong, respected, and open, the students responded positively. Not many students could have pulled that off. But Dick did because he had respectfully interacted with so many diverse personalities and groups. If the media would allow them, maybe some of our political leaders could take a few lessons from Dick. That is, maybe they, too, could practice honest and truthful interaction without the fear of negative and twisted stories splashing across various headlines.

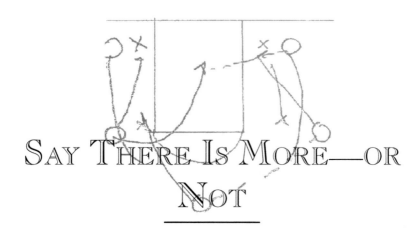

Say There Is More—or Not

It was one of my first experiences coaching at the high school level. I had just completed my student teaching and was anxious to begin my career at a new school in a large city. I was going to have an opportunity to coach junior varsity basketball at a 4A level. I was excited and a bit apprehensive. I was particularly concerned about the difficult task of sorting through prospective athletes to come up with a workable team. I was not excited about choosing which individuals would make the team and which would be asked to compete elsewhere or turn out for another sport. The term *cut* has always left a sour or bitter taste in my mouth.

Over fifty young men showed up for the first practice. The trouble is, this was the only turnout for three levels. It did not take a genius to figure out that this was a meager number. We hoped that the turnout would increase the following day. The next day's numbers did change, but not as we had hoped. Unfortunately, our number decreased. We lost three seniors who had decided not to turn out. What made matters even worse is that there were twenty-one freshmen turning out. That left a total of twenty-six players for the varsity and JV. The varsity kept twelve players and "cut" three seniors. That left a total of eleven players turning out for the JV team. Needless to say, we decided to keep all eleven players.

Despite the low numbers, I began to practice with great enthusiasm. Six of the players showed some skill and had played a little basketball before. Our tallest players were six feet one inch and six feet two inches, and we possessed only average speed. We lacked experience, size, and skill. In addition, we had a rookie coach that was excited, but untested. What made it even worse, two of the players had flunked the section on basketball in PE class.

Despite these hurdles, the players and I looked forward to our first game. We were anxious to test the waters and get a barometer of where we were. During the warm-ups, my jaw must have dropped as I watched six of the opposing players dunk the ball. In contrast, I knew we would be lucky if we had a person who could grab the rim. Still, our hard work, intensity, and strategy would compensate for some of our physical shortcomings. Without belaboring a painful situation, we ended up getting "edged" by the score of 87-28. I was devastated. This was not supposed to have happened.

The next day in practice, I noticed that the players did not have a defeatist or different attitude from our preseason practices. They carried on with the same focus and intensity. I was taken aback. They must have accepted their demise and become complacent. Or maybe we had run into a juggernaut the first game and would regroup and realize our potential in our next game.

Three days later, we played our second game. "It was much better." The final score read 86-29. We had scored twenty-two points in the second half against their second and third strings. We had scored a total of seven points in the first half. To make matters worse for our fragile egos, the freshman squad was 2-0 and playing at a very tough level. I thought against arranging a scrimmage between the freshmen and JV teams. It would be a no-win situation for the JVs and could damage egos that were balanced between hard and determined play—and insecurity. Instead, we decided to focus on improvement and not on the scoreboard. We really did not have any other choice. I realized quickly that we had a long road to travel and John Wooden did not need to worry about his job.

Even though the varsity had not won a game, I realized that there probably was very little likeliness that any of my "stars" would be pulled up to the varsity level. The scores slowly started to improve. We lost one game by eighteen points. We kept focusing on our goals and improvement and became very positive with each other. We developed a reputation of a fiery team that had a "no quit" attitude. Opposing coaches would come up to me after the game and always comment about our intensity, enthusiasm, and overall effort. Of course, most of the time these comments are reserved for teams that you feel sorry for and are trying to give them a ray of hope.

Maybe we were just fooling ourselves. Yet the enthusiasm was infectious, and I found myself respecting all of the team members. To this day, each member has a special place in my memory bank. We were 0-14, and I was enjoying these young men. They had such a healthy spin on competition. They took games in perspective and approached each game with hopes that were tempered with realism.

We were meeting a team that only defeated us by twenty-two points the first time. Even though our games were getting closer, we had not even had an opportunity to "choke." No game had been even remotely close to cause pressure. We entered the game on a positive note. We jumped ahead 6-2. Unfortunately, the opposition closed out the quarter by scoring sixteen unanswered points. We had fallen behind by twelve points, and it seemed as if we were going to follow the same old pattern, playing the reserves in the fourth quarter to make it look a bit better. But slowly, the game turned. Our pressing defense started turning into converted baskets. It was unbelievable, but we had closed the gap to four points at the end of the half. We kept up the pressure, and despite fouling out two starters, we stayed in the game and were only behind by five points two minutes into the fourth quarter. Suddenly, the momentum shifted, and we found ourselves down by eleven with four minutes left in the game. Wally came to the bench during a time-out screaming at the top of his lungs. "We have fought too hard to let it go this way!" he yelled. It was as if we got another shot of adrenaline. The lead started dwindling, and we were closing in on a possible win. With one minute left, we were only down by three points. We stole the ball four straight times and successfully converted. We scored the last nine points to close out a six-point victory.

We closed out the season by winning five out of our last seven games. All involved noted the improvement, and those five wins were sweet to say the least. But the heart and grit was shown in those two games we lost.

We were playing a team that had beaten us earlier by over fifty points. We had high hopes going into the second game. We had actually won two straight games and were hoping for a miracle win. We gamely fought through the first half but pathetically trailed by a score of 47-16. Our half-time talk dealt with a little strategy, but moreover, we questioned if we had any more reserve to reach down to. Could we give more? What followed was one of the most emotional experiences of my educational and athletic career. These players gave more as a unit than I have ever witnessed. They crashed into walls, dove in the bleachers, scraped skin on the floor numerous times. They gave so much; not one player walked off the court at the end of the game unscathed. Bloodstained, drenched in sweat, and virtually no energy left, these men were truly warriors. They were representative of what we all strive for—all heart and grit. Even though we lost by a score of 76-71, it was truly one of the most inspiring efforts I have seen. The players were rewarded with a standing ovation from over three hundred opposing fans. They had experienced a Herculean effort by these young men. After the game, I was choked with emotion and could hardly speak. I could only thank these men for such a determined and no-quit effort.

The second game had a completely different twist. The best team in the league was solidly beating us. Although the final score was a fifteen-point loss, it truly was a much-sounder whipping. During the fourth quarter, a player who had not ever competed in a sport before this season and was one of the individuals who had failed PE basketball stepped to the free throw line. Now he was 0-14 for the season from the field, and this only was his fifth attempt at a free throw. Earlier in the season he had hit the upper corner of the backboard on one free throw and got nothing but air on the second. Down by twenty points at this time he calmly took aim at the basket. He shot, and it hit nothing but the net. The bench erupted, and three of his best buddies ran on to the court and picked him up in the air. The joy was genuine and the congratulations sincere, for they had always treated this individual with respect. We immediately were assessed three technical fouls. I was embarrassed and yet so proud. These players had completely lost themselves to congratulate their successful buddy. The rest of the team was wildly cheering. After the commotion settled down, he calmly sank his second free throw. A minute later, he hit a fifteen-foot shot from the baseline. I am sure that he will have fond memories of that game for the rest of his life. At the end of the game, the ref came up to me and said he was sorry that he had to assess the technical fouls. "But you know Coach, that was the most inspiring moment I have ever witnessed as a ref. Your kids not only have heart, they are truly a team," he added.

These players again had demonstrated an unselfish pride in their team and its members. They were one of the most successful teams I have ever coached. Not in terms of win-losses, but in terms of guts, determination, intensity, and improvement. These characteristics have carried over into their family and professional lives. To a man, each person is a success according to society's standards; but more importantly, they are playing the game of life on their own terms and reaping a deeper level of satisfaction.

ARE YOU LAUGHING NOW?

During the first few years of being a head basketball coach, I felt compelled to give my freshman coach an opportunity to choose which individuals would stay on the team. We would discuss certain individuals, but for the most part I trusted his decisions. However, a near-critical mistake changed my view.

For three years, we had not had a prospective female athlete over five feet ten inches tall. We finally had a young lady named Shirley, who was almost six feet tall. When the day came for final decisions for the Frosh team to be finalized, I asked the coach which fifteen people on the team would receive uniforms. He quickly rattled off a list of his top fifteen players. "Ah, Coach, I see that Shirley is not on your list," I stated. "Yeah, she has real bad feet, is uncoordinated, and does not possess a temperament for the game," he replied. "Because she is big and tough, I want this young lady in our program," I retorted. He was an open and objective individual, who was not taken by himself, so consequently he agreed with the decision to give her an extended stay. Even though this coach was one of the best I have ever been associated with, since that time, we decided that a coach's committee should choose all three levels.

Within three weeks, it was obvious that she belonged in our program. Although demonstrating the grace of a yearling, she was tough and could move. We decided to move her to the JV team where there were fewer players, and she would receive much more playing time. By the end of the season, the only time she was on the bench was when she was in foul trouble. Although she would miss numerous put-back shots and layins, because of very little refinement in her game, this awkward-looking player seemed to have the necessary superior movement and hand-eye coordination to lay the foundation for her to become an impact player.

During the off season, after the completion of our summer league games, each player would receive a workout card designed specifically to improve deficient and particular skills. Each workout would take between thirty and sixty minutes to complete. Most players would complete the workout two or three times a week. I am sure that some never ventured out to complete the workout. But there were a few who diligently worked out and would go far beyond expectations.

Although not a requirement, all players were encouraged to call me to help them with their workouts. But after the grueling summer was completed, few chose to harass the old coach. I would give the girls this choice because I felt that after a long and tedious summer of games and tournaments, I wanted the player to initiate the workout herself. This placed ownership on the player and offered proof of a genuine desire to improve and honest love for the game.

Once Shirley made the first phone call, she found it easy to request help each time. Sometimes she would call as many as three times a week. We would work hard to develop a variety of jump shots, hooks, and moves.

Other times she wanted to go play against the "male hoop hounds" that frequented the many outdoor courts.

Now, I must admit, that I loved playing during the summer on outdoor courts. Taking one, two, or three girls on an evening or a weekend to play against three or four male "hoopers" was beneficial and enjoyable. Most of the time, we would "keep the court" and then, be challenged by some other group. Unfortunately, this could be devastating to some of the fragile egos of the "hoop hounds." I imagine their hearts would sink when they would see us walking on the court.

One weekend we were playing a group of four we had played a number of other times. The game was close, and another team was waiting on the sidelines to challenge the winner. As usual, the play was intense and physical. All of a sudden, there was a loud voice screaming swear words and distinct adjectives from the baseline. One of the larger "hounds" had grabbed Shirley by the collar and was threatening to "bust her up, girl or no girl." His teammates quickly subdued and pulled him away. When I got to Shirley, it was obvious that she was noticeably shook up. "Coach, I have no idea why he is so upset. I was just blocking out on the boards like you have taught us," she stammered. Now, when Shirley would block out on the boards, she would truly block out on the boards. I know because I have a rearranged nose from one of her efforts. It was also obvious that this hound was probably embarrassed and frustrated.

"Let's go over to the other court and work on some moves or play two by two for a while," I said. Quietly and with some hesitation, she said, "I would like to finish this game." The score was tied when the game resumed. She was noticeably shaken, but responded like a true competitor by making two great moves to finish the game.

The young man did come up later and apologize. "Hey, things like that happen during the heat of competition," she said.

I believe she understood his frustration in this male-dominated domain and was trying to ease his pain.

After that, Shirley even stepped up her workouts. She now became a leader by example. This inspiration on the court fired competitive juices in her teammates. This fire and intensity partly contributed to a streak of forty-four straight league wins over a two-and-one-half-year period.

Shirley had now become one of the most dominating players in the league. She basically refused to let us lose. We were trying to maintain this streak of wins going into the last game of her senior year. We were playing the second place team on their home court. We had sewn up the league title two games earlier, but the streak was still on the line. One of our top scorers was unable to play because of an injury. Also, the opposing team came out tough with an upbeat and an intense level of play. In the third quarter, Shirley turned an already tender and heavily taped ankle. She limped to the bench and sat down in frustration. Tears were welling up in her eyes because of the pain and disappointment. The trainer informed me that her return to play would be highly painful and unlikely.

With the score tied, one of the other key players fouled out at the end of the third quarter. Within the first minute of the fourth quarter, our deficit had risen to six points. "Coach, I am ready to play," Shirley said. "There is no need for you to play. We will tough it out and see where the pieces will fall," I answered. "It is not worth the risk of further injury," I continued. She put her head in her hands and began to cry. "I have always wanted to finish this year undefeated, and I have worked so hard . . . ," her voice was trailing off. "This is my number 1 goal. Please let me finish," she added. The trainer agreed, and I reluctantly put her in for the last six minutes. You could feel it in the air as she limped on the court. We were about to witness something very rare and unique.

She started out by blocking two shots in a row. She grabbed the ball and fired an outlet pass. She then rebounded the miss and stuck it back for a three-point play. She then stole the inbounds pass and quickly scored again. Her seventeen-foot fade-away winning shot at the buzzer hit nothing but the net. She garnered eleven rebounds, had three steals, and scored fifteen points in the last six minutes. It truly was one of the most unbelievable athletic feats I have ever witnessed at any level in any sport.

Being chosen MVP at the state tournament topped off her year. This followed a miserable showing at the state tournament the year before. She proved, beyond any shadow of a doubt, what diligence, hard work, and heart can accomplish if you truly want it and believe. My hat goes off to this warrior of heart and courage.

DON'T STEP ON MY LIP

I was quietly grading papers one morning prior to school when a young girl came busting through the door. "Coach, coach," she gasped between breaths. "We have a new freshman basketball player, and, Coach, she can really play," she exclaimed enthusiastically. I have never gotten too excited about advertised players. Most of the time, they are flash in the pans or "buffoons." I calmly looked up and said, "We will see when 'showtime' arrives." I had heard about this young girl named Lindsey, who was a younger sister in one of the most recognized athletic families in the area. Yet, so much of the time, reputations can be more detrimental than beneficial. So I waited with guarded anticipation for the opening days of basketball practice. Lindsey and I chatted informally a number of times before tryouts began. I noted that she never bragged or baited for compliments. She seemed reluctant to talk about herself. She was friendly and open, but would almost become embarrassed if the conversations were about her. There definitely was no "buffoonery" in this young lady.

By the second day of practice, all of the coaches were truly impressed with the raw talent Lindsey demonstrated. She had unbelievable hand-eye coordination, could run and jump out of the gym. She was energetic and freely interacted and complimented her older peers. Although rough around the edges, she picked up fundamentals, through drills, faster than any player I have ever coached. She also demonstrated superior intelligence and athletic sense.

From the start we knew that this young lady was a special player. Despite her freshman status, Lindsey played the entire season at the varsity level. She was the sixth or seventh player in the first eight games of the season. After that, she became a full-time starter. She was tough, talented, and team oriented to a fault. For example, on a number of occasions, she would stop shooting because she felt that her fellow teammates deserved their accolades. But she had one serious flaw. When faced with adversity, she may feel that she had failed her team and would pout, stop, and hang her head. Benching her seemed pointless; in that she would be happy to sit on the bench and cheer for her team. Unfortunately, we were not nearly as successful with her on the bench.

When I challenged her about her behavior on the court, she appeared both frustrated and confused. "I know that acting like that only can hurt the team, but I just can't seem to break the habit," she mumbled. "I have always responded that way when I get upset," she added. She seemed open to help in overcoming the problem. We designed various strategies to help her. Over the next four weeks, she showed a slight improvement. We finally decided on two key power words that would hopefully trigger awareness in her, and she would snap out of the funk. I would shout these words to her, and she was to respond. Eventually, Lindsey became conditioned and would quickly respond in a favorable manner.

Lindsey led the team to a four-year winning record of 87 percent. But over that time span, there were a few more obstacles she had to overcome. Although Lindsey still struggled with periods of excessive self-criticism, she still was a dynamic and an influential leader. This leadership was not defined specifically until her senior year. But moreover, it was subtle and indirect. Her timely humor and excellent physical ability powered her role. The team was strongly influenced by her dynamic personality. Her free spirit, hilarious sense of humor, and general gregarious relationships with her peers put a skew and spirit to the team that was invigorating and refreshing. True, her skill was a trigger for inspiration to team members, but her winning smile and genuine concern for others added the necessary stability.

Yet there still was a lot of room for growth. As a player, her skills developed with speed and refinement. From mastering a jump shot in less than ten practices, to behind the back dribbles at full speed, to eye-popping drives, she truly was poetry in motion. She was tough on defense, possessed all the physical attributes, and had great understanding of the game and overall goals. She led the team in steals (four years), points (three years), and rebounds (two years) and was second in assists. But her self-critical and perfectionist attitude was a major obstacle that she continuously had to battle. On one occasion she had experienced frustration during the first quarter of play. Her quick hands had given her two quick fouls. Lindsey's hand and foot speed defied the norm. So many times she would accomplish things that seemed impossible for referees to accept. So they would whistle fouls unjustly. She went into her funk. The lip dropped, and she retreated to a slow jog. She was immediately pulled from the game. I thought to myself, *No, not again.* We slowly lost our slim lead. Down by four points with three minutes left in the half, I took a gamble and sent her back in the game. As she approached the bench, her sagging shoulders and poor eye contact indicated a questionable performance. What followed was embarrassing to her teammates, herself, and me. She loafed, refused to shoot, and came up empty on the boards. Her teammates tried in vain to make up for the void she had created. In disgust, I pulled her with just less than a minute left in the half.

Now Lindsey and I had a solid coach-to-player as well as student-to-teacher relationship. I felt I could be honest and open with her. However, I never tried to humiliate a player in front of their peers. As we were solemnly walking to the locker room, I was confused, frustrated, and angry. *After all we had worked on, how could she do this to her team?* I asked myself. I have never before or since chastised a player like I did Lindsey. "I have never seen a worse display of childish and self-centered play exhibited by a player!" I shouted. "You are an embarrassment to your team, its players, and the school as a whole," I screeched. As Lindsey hung her head, this verbal challenge continued throughout the half-time break. As she left the locker room, she refused to give me eye contact as the tears poured down her face.

Lindsey did not start the second half. She was forced to sit right next to me. After a few minutes, I leaned over and said, "Are you ready to play or embarrass the team even more?" She stared straight ahead and nodded. "No nods, I need a promise," I barked. She calmly looked at me and said, "I promise I will play hard." As she briskly walked to the scorer's table, I felt a drastic change was about to happen. She completely changed her approach and, consequently, her impact on the game. Rarely have I ever witnessed a more intense level of play. In just over thirteen minutes of play, she scored twenty-two points and garnered fifteen rebounds. It truly was an amazing display of basketball. Her dynamic play spearheaded us to a fifteen-point victory.

Lindsey was mad at the situation, herself, and me. She did not speak at all during the bus ride home. She quickly exited the bus, went to the locker room, and quietly strolled to the bus stop. I could not help but wonder what would be going through her head during the bus ride home. The next day I called her to my room. I could tell that she was still stinging from the verbal chastising by her aloof demeanor. "Lindsey, we have got to figure out how to avoid the type of behavior you displayed yesterday from occurring again," I said. She did not do a very good job of covering her frustration and anger. After a long period of silence, she blurted out, "I'm tired of trying. I always seem to fall back into the same rut. It seems so pointless. But since you don't give up on me, I won't give up on myself. I'll do whatever it takes . . . ," her voice was trailing off. It was evident that this problem was not going to leave or disappear with a few gimmicks. But doggedly she kept bouncing back and trying.

During her junior year, we had a few weeks before state when Lindsey fell into a funk during practice. I was experiencing some stress because the next two games were essential to secure the league championship and an automatic berth to the state tournament. Her tantrum had come at a very key time in practice. In disgust I called everyone up to the baseline to run sets. However, there was one little catch. We were running for Lindsey. Since she was unable to handle her own actions or responsibilities, the team would do it for her. She was to sit on the floor and watch everyone else run for her. There was one other little catch: the sets would not count if she ran with them. It left a lasting impact because we only had to do this one more time before we finally eliminated an ugly habit.

Lindsey had endured so much to break this habit that I could not help but admire her resilience and internal fortitude. It took a persistent and tough individual to break such a strong and consuming habit.

So often we express our deep personal frustrations by pointing fingers at others, rationalizing our actions or giving up entirely. It is refreshing to see individuals accept responsibility for their actions and change without sacrificing values or principles. I feel fortunate to have coached an individual as talented as Lindsey. Not just because of her physical skills. But because she was and is a person who had solid values, perceptivity, and the guts to struggle for change.

Maybe Quality Does Count

Despite being a paced group, this class had a curiosity about subject matter and a genuine desire to learn. Their academic skills were weak and underdeveloped. But their perceptivity and intelligence were strong as indicated by their enthusiastic and energetic questions, debates, and discussions. But moreover, they had that most essential quality called curiosity.

Assignments and quizzes had indicated a mixed bag of achievements. Some students met, and a few even exceeded expectations. But most of them struggled just to meet minimum standards. Despite their inconsistent level of achievement, I felt that the true intrinsic desire to learn would catapult most to success on their unit tests. I decided to administer the same test to the paced and regular classes. I felt that this sincere and enthusiastic desire to learn would be a springboard to success.

Test day can create anxiety for teachers, as well as students. The risk I was taking could hurt or dampen the enthusiasm they had previously shown. It also reflected, in part, my effectiveness as a teacher. All of the students had accepted the challenge and diligently prepared. My anxiety was at such a pitch that I found it difficult to sleep the previous night. When they entered the room on test day, there seemed to be a strong feeling of confidence. All of the students worked until the end of the period. Some even chose to stay through their lunch to complete the test. They seemed to have a sense of confidence and accomplishment as they handed in their tests.

As I began to grade the papers, I was pleased to note that the first two students had scored over 80 percent. Unfortunately, the grades plunged downward after that. After I calculated the class average, I was crushed and challenged my decision to administer a difficult test. The average was 38 percent. This compared to a 75 percent and 72 percent average by the regular classes. I knew that I had overestimated their ability to retain information or take a test. In either case, I had to accept the responsibility for a faulty judgment.

When I handed the tests back the following day, there were shocked faces throughout the room. We went over the test, and many students expressed frustration over their missed questions. Most of the mistakes came from an incomplete or misread question. Seven of the students scored below 20 percent. Stan was devastated when he saw his 13-percent score. "I know the answers, I just freeze when I try to put the answers down on paper," he exclaimed. Many students will use such excuses to avoid responsibility. But Stan and the rest of the class did not seem to fall into that category. After discussing the causes and possible solutions, the class unanimously decided to give it another shot. Nobody wanted to have a "watered down" version of the test. Secondly, they wanted to move at the same pace as the regular classes. One student exclaimed loudly, "Don't make it easy on us, we'll step up and meet the challenge."

The mutual effort and cooperation was inspiring for me as a teacher to note. Not only were these students anxious to learn and participate, they truly were concerned about grades and level of achievement. We worked hard on studying techniques, retention, and application of material. We created study groups, created note cards with questions and answers, and established challenge groups. It was as if an athletic team was preparing for its next contest.

The next test created anticipation and excitement. The students put in extra hours studying after school. After the test, students again expressed confidence. And the results were encouraging. The average score was 57 percent. If we took out the bottom two scores, it was 65 percent.

Even though he improved seven points to 20 percent, Stan was devastated after receiving his test. "You know, Mr. Mac, I still feel I know the material," he mumbled. I asked Stan where he felt the problem was founded. "I do not know, but I do feel hurried and rushed," he replied. Stan was one of the most knowledgeable and conscientious students in the class. I just hated to see him suffer and receive unjust grades. He was perceptive, well organized, and intuitive. But for some reason, his test anxiety kept him from proving his knowledge.

I believe that tests are not foolproof in measuring learning or knowledge; however, it may be the fairest and most revealing. Because academic or intellectual inferiority or failure is taboo, we try to soft-soap or water down challenges. We fool ourselves into thinking a person understands through subjective evaluation. What we should be doing is tightening up our bootstraps and developing strategies that help a student raise expectations and achievement level. Let's not lower our standards, but rather lead them in meeting the challenge. The students in this class reinforced this philosophy by expressing a concern about not selling them short.

However, I saw that Stan was beginning to question his own worth and ability. Maybe I was expecting too much from him. He came to me before school to discuss this frustration and possible options. We discussed his style, talents, and potential. "I feel that I have been pigeonholed into slow groups in my years of school. I have been in paced classes for years. But I can deal with any subject. You can ask me any question about what we have been studying, and I will know the answer," he stated strongly. As we reviewed his test, we saw that he had left large portions of questions blank. He had only partially answered a few other questions. Almost all of his answers were either incomplete or blank. So we decided that he should not leave any questions unanswered. He would also complete each answer before moving on to the next question. He seemed relieved to know that a strategy was created to take the pressure of time off his shoulders.

During our next test, I noticed that Stan was very focused. When the bell rang for the completion of the class, a few stayed extra minutes to complete their test. I wandered by to take note of Stan's progress. He had only completed one of a five-page test. "Would it be okay if I work through lunch?" he asked. Yet even after lunch, he was only through with his second page. I then picked up his test and asked him to come in after school to finish. He arrived immediately after school. After two more hours of work, he finally completed his test. He wanted to wait while I graded his test. I believe we both felt a high degree of anxiety as I carefully graded each question. We celebrated with a "high five" after I calculated his score and wrote 92 percent at the top of the page.

We finally had discovered Stan's problem. He was a perfectionist. If answers were not perfectly organized and complete, he would become anxious and unable to complete the questions. Then anxiety and frustration would block any efficient work. He just needed more time to complete his tests.

A few days later Stan came to me and said it was unfair for him to have additional time on a test. Consequently, a new opportunity was provided for all students. I would come two hours earlier in the morning of test days. Any student who wanted could get an early jump on the test. Only Stan and one other student took advantage of this opportunity. Most students did not need the additional time. Stan never got below a 95 percent on a test the rest of the year. He eventually made arrangements with other teachers. The next year he was moved completely out of the paced group. His grades changed from Cs to As.

Eventually, Stan applied and received at scholarship at a prestigious university. He graduated with honors and went on to get his masters and doctorate degrees. This all came about because he would not accept his failure. Here was a young man who had been labeled as inferior or academically challenged—receiving honors in college and moving to the highest levels of education. He now works for a large chemical corporation. And of course, he volunteers time to tutor students struggling in school.

I Have Another Side

I had just recently accepted a position as a teacher and coach at a school in a different state. The environment, system, and school were new; and I had very little previous knowledge of any circumstances concerning the athletic structure and personnel. I was also unfamiliar with the personality and athletic ability of the various aspiring participants. However, a few helpful colleagues were anxious to offer diverse insight and perspective. They gave brief or, in some cases, detailed backgrounds about individuals and experiences. While these were informative and provided me with a solid base of understanding, there seemed to be a few areas that had some division of views.

Although there were some small areas of disagreement, most of the conclusions about one individual centered on some basic characteristics. It seemed that there was a consensus that Brandon was selfish, dishonest, and disrespectful. Each person would add something about the basic athletic ability of this one individual. They would also follow the statement with a discouraging lament about a waste of untapped potential. Yet during spring camp I noted how his quick and thorough thinking lent itself to clearer understanding of detail and overall schemes. His questions were directed with purpose in hopes of gaining a clearer and complete understanding of goals and methods. Because of this demonstration, I felt that he could have a positive influence on all members of the team.

During the summer of that initial season, I had various opportunities to discuss the role of many of the individuals on the team. Brandon and I had numerous meetings to discuss leadership, positive attitude, and modeling discipline and character. It seemed as if he understood its importance for reaching potential and team success. As a quarterback, it was critical for him to always encourage, be positively intense, and possess a clear understanding of the offense and desired role for each individual. He mastered these, as well as any athlete I have ever coached. What was even more exciting was how quickly he understood how important it was for leaders to step forward in the face of adversity. A successful team is, in part, predicated on the ability of the leaders to stabilize and motivate a group when the foundation has been shaken. He quickly learned to use positive reinforcement to strengthen the mental makeup of the team when faced with doubt, uncertainty, or failure. He would either use intensity or "cool" when he noted anxiety and frustration growing. Along with five or six others, he helped lead this team to unexpected success.

Brandon began to change his previously perceived image. Fellow team members began to respect his demeanor, knowledge, and intensity. He placed the welfare of the team over selfish and superficial roles. And at no time during the season did he exemplify anything but class and poise.

But this is not really about the field leadership or success. The real quality goes so much deeper and helps all of us refocus our perspective and goals. The dynamics of this story really begins one year before I took this new job. A tragedy had occurred prior to the beginning of summer workouts. One late night in June, a popular and talented young football player's life was suddenly taken in a violent automobile accident. Many players on the team had not only lost a tough competitor, but a very close friend. The ensuing season apparently was marked with shattered dreams and team frustrations. But the memory of this individual stayed ever so strongly in the hearts and minds of a number of these young men.

I stumbled onto the gravity of this traumatic event one evening during the summer. I had finished painting a mural on the weight room wall. It was a football scene that depicted a ball carrier being tackled by three opposing players. The following evening I had to take a trip home to arrange some final details of the upcoming move. Another coach had agreed to supervise the weight room for two evenings. When I got back a few days later, I was shocked and disappointed. Apparently, one or more had vandalized my painting. Somebody had found the paint in the back storage area and had "painted out" one of the player's uniform. It distorted and cheapened the picture. I was livid. How could anybody disfigure a painting that was given only to help make the room more appealing? That evening during weight training, I expressed my deep displeasure and frustration. After everyone else had left for the evening, Brandon came to me and confessed. He seemed both intense and embarrassed. He stammered for a few moments before finally giving an explanation. Apparently, the number on the player who was carrying the ball was the number of the deceased teammate. I still remember his words, "Coach, it was wrong to change the painting, but I wanted to honor his memory and keep our promise. His number was unofficially retired," he said.

There was a long period of silence before any other words were spoken. Eventually, we discussed the matter in greater detail. We decided that there had to be a more appropriate way of solving a problem. And although I did not appreciate what he did, I had nothing but respect for why he did it.

Although we had pulled one major upset and were playing well, our season had gotten off to a "rocky start." Despite being 1-3, the players seemed to play with a purpose and intensity. We were at the midpoint of our season when we finally got a break from league play. We were to play a nonleague rival. The players were intense, and the emotional level was high and electric. Despite a sound thrashing at home the previous year, our players walked onto the field with purpose and intensity. They were excited and anxious to establish themselves and gain respect. The night was cold, and the thin wisps of fog would make brief periodic appearances that were only cosmetic in nature. The excitement was high, and the large fan participation added flavor to the evening. The game was a battle. The score seesawed back and forth. As time was winding down, we made a few desperate attempts in the last minute to break a tie. However, the inevitable happened—overtime. After they scored and failed on the extra point, we had our chance. On fourth down, we completed a pass for a first down at the one-foot line. However, the back official overruled the completion. Our players were stunned and bitter. It seemed as if this game was plucked right from our hands. The video confirmed the catch. The players had worked so hard and had fallen just short. There were tears of frustration that only deserved individuals have a right to feel. Even though we had failed to reach our goal on the scoreboard, our self-respect and dignity wavered only so slightly.

The boys dressed in relative silence. Those who had given so much should only share in this silence. I feel that mutual pain felt after an honorable struggle is a privilege to be shared by only the most dedicated individuals. Most of the players had left the locker room. There was quiet over the room that is only noted when a bitter loss is punctuated with intense effort and sacrifice. Brandon came to me quietly and made a very unusual request. It seemed that their teammate had had his accident only about ten miles from the school. Brandon asked if we could stop the bus so that some of the players could offer their respects. I quietly agreed.

The bus was relatively quiet. There was the usual discussion about the game and a few players relived the stress by quietly offering a humorous remark or two. We had arranged for the driver to stop in a turnaround about seventy-five yards from where the accident had occurred. The bus slowly ground to a halt, and complete silence fell over the team. Only about twelve players had worked closely with this individual before his untimely death. One by one, these twelve individuals got up and quietly made their way to the front of the bus. The other players on the bus knew that this was a time that had a very special meaning to these young men. They sat in the dark in complete silence while the players made their way over to the spot of the deadly crash.

In the darkness of the evening, we could barely make out the shadows as they slowly knelt down and bowed their heads. After a few minutes, they made their way back to the bus. Quietly, each person climbed aboard with sullen faces and tears in their eyes. The rest of the team said nothing. It was a special time, a time to offer respect and love for a fallen friend. It seemed as if all team members and coaches knew it was a frozen moment in time that did not need commentary. A unique and special bond was built that evening: A bond that meant more than any game or scoreboard. This team had discovered a level that went far beyond the lights, fame, and status that oftentimes accompanies success. The unity created by that evening provided these young men with a sense of brotherhood.

It was very late, and there were not any fast-food restaurants open to grab a meal before the trip home. However, we did stop at a grocery store so that the players could get something to satisfy their hunger temporarily. As I was searching the shelves for anything that looked palatable, Brandon came to me and asked another question. One of our players was just getting off academic probation and would begin playing in the game the next week. He asked a question that I am sure related to our win-loss record up to that point. He humbly asked if I was going to make a change at quarterback. This was an unlikely question coming from a person who had given and grown so much. But I guess it was a reflection of his primary thoughts about team and group success. My response was simple, and I smiled as I said, "No, Brandon, I am not a fool. You have given so much of yourself, and we are starting to roll." I added, "If it ain't broke, don't fix it." He nodded and quietly thanked me. He then quickly turned and walked toward the door of the store.

The remainder of the season was exciting and successful. We won our final five league games and made it to the second round of the state tournament. I believe that the foundation of that team was solidified that evening when a group of men made their way to a dimly lit intersection to show respect and love for their fallen teammate. It is evident that the unique experience helped forge a bond of unity and unselfishness that is still cherished by all team members and coaching staff.

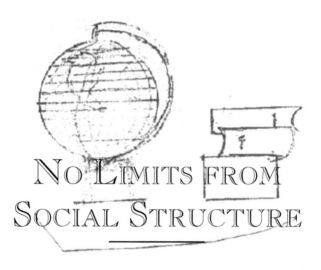

No Limits from Social Structure

Some people have described education as bittersweet or counterproductive. The teaching field presents numerous challenges and contradictions. Teachers are expected to wear different hats and play numerous roles in hopes of motivating our students. Rules, standards, and improved performance, oftentimes, conflict with individuality and creativity. Numerous times, it has been stated to my students that schools or formal education can be stumbling blocks to creativity and learning. The pressures from the outside community, to note or see results, force educators to structure measurement of growth and learning through tests or exams. There seems to be solid reasoning behind this concept. First of all, exams or tests seem to be the most thorough and objective means of evaluation. Secondly, students are highly motivated when they can note growth and performance through a numerical score. Yet we do not want to "can" tests for fear of losing extensive depth and applied learning.

Also, we are told to not hurt or inhibit personal growth by drawing comparisons of students. Teachers are told to minimize the competition between students. Yet the standards or grades are based off comparisons or curves of a certain group of people. Oftentimes, a conflict between high motivation and expectations and the establishment of a secure self-image can develop.

Our society stresses the virtues of competition. Idealistically, people will compete to improve performance and make new and better products to benefit the society as a whole. We mouth fair play and hard work. Yet we know that dishonest and lazy people can "win" a battle because of luck, talent, intelligence, or deceit. It is obvious that the skepticism that educators have regarding tests and test score comparisons has some merit.

We need to create fair and objective means of evaluation as tools for increased performance and motivation as well as documentation. It is true that as students begin to compete with each other, some begin to "pygmalionize" themselves and others into certain academic categories or pigeonholes. Consequently, I have found that competing against your best self brings about high motivation and results without establishing a "cut throat" atmosphere. Students can note their progress and make adjustments to ensure better performance. The key is to inspire students to set goals that are just barely within their reach. This is a critical step in motivating students to increase their knowledge and skill.

In many of my classes, students were told to predict a score for their next test. Prior to this prediction, a two-day lesson dealing with expectations of others and us is given. Students are told not to undersell themselves. Since we seem to expect 100 percent from a mechanic, doctor, lawyer, etc., how can we expect less than 100 percent out of ourselves without being a hypocrite? Students then are told to give the highest scores they think that they can reach. Anything under 70 percent is not acceptable.

After proper direction, every student has given a score over 70 percent with most scores predicted being over 95 percent. Three out of four students reach their goals. Also, any student may try to take a harder test later. The two scores would then be averaged.

Carol was a person who demanded the most out of herself. She felt that cheating was an indication of weakness or ignorance. On one occasion, we debated for twenty-five minutes after class about a test score. She felt that she did not deserve the score of 98 percent. She felt it should be a score of 94 percent. She felt that this score was not accurate and undeserving. Carol believed that any score not earned was an insult to a person's integrity and intelligence. "I would not give you additional points of undeserved; likewise, I will not grade you down because of your overt self-criticism," I said. "I believe you need to be tougher when grading my papers," she countered. So for the rest of the year, I would search diligently to grade her down for any slight mistake I could find. This seemed to lessen her opposition and allow her to focus on goals.

On another occasion, the students were given the opportunity to take a test over again. As mentioned before, an average of the two scores would determine the final grade for that test. Carol had received a grade of 99 percent on the test. Although I did not ask Carol and three other students, most of the class chose to take advantage of the opportunity. Carol raised her hand and asked why she was not given the opportunity to take the test again. I explained that taking another test could not really increase test scores of 98 or 99. She emphatically countered by using my own words, "Mr. Mac, I always expect 100 percent from others such as doctors or mechanics. Why should I not demand 100 percent from myself? Touché—her point was well taken, and she was allowed to take a much harder test. After careful criticism and deliberation over her test, I had to give her a score of 100.

Today Carol is a doctor of medicine. And no—she does not suffer from a perfectionist personality. But she will always play the game straight and demand 100 percent from herself. She is open and freely interacts on a personal basis with all people. There is no doubt that any one of us would want a person of such high goals and personal integrity to serve or help us in any capacity. I am sure she demands the same professional and personal quality from herself that she exhibited as a student. I have nothing but admiration for a person who demands so much from themselves and goes beyond the restraints of society. She is truly an unsung hero with all the key ingredients for personal and professional success.

You Only Know Part of Me

Any athletic endeavor requires a mix of concentration and confidence. Every individual has methods ranging from subtle to extreme in hopes of maximizing potential. Oftentimes there is such a slight margin that determines what is so often called success. I wonder how many times the margin that separated failure and success depended on the ability to mentally focus before the contest. Each individual, organization, and the sport itself determine the various methods used for preparation. But there is no doubt that focus can have great impact on a player or team reaching potential.

Emotions can vary from sport to sport. In sports such as football, basketball, soccer, and volleyball, adrenaline and aggression need to be emitted and channeled. Teams and players do everything from playing upbeat music, practice repetitive rituals and superstitions, emit yells and chants in unison, and exhibit all forms of body language to hype fellow teammates. There is no doubt that group attitude and overall atmosphere can be effective springboards to superior performance. The question is whether or not the hype is short-lived, helps with concentration, or can be sustained and utilized throughout the entire competition.

Yet each individual is different and have developed their own style to help with mental focus and overall performance. Kyle's preparation for football games was different, but not entirely unique. While various leaders made verbal and nonverbal gestures to create an atmosphere of intensity, a few seemed quietly focused. Sometimes we, as coaches, misinterpret the style used by a certain group or individual. More often than not, the intensity and adrenaline levels were probably quite similar, yet the methods used were very different. Kyle, like a few others, would give us a familiar sight. Even though not usual, a number of times I have seen those riveted eyes gleam with competitive anticipation. The stares were almost icy in nature. But the souls behind the stares were alive and focused. Kyle's steely glare and focused body language had a powerful influence on fellow team members. And when he stepped into the huddle to speak, his teammates became silent and intently listened to his stern, quiet, and succinct message.

I remember on two different occasions, we were playing big games that would require extraordinary effort and heart. On one occasion we were playing far below our ability. As coaches, we had orchestrated, what we believed to be, a highly motivated and inspirational pregame speech. However, our response to first-half adversity had dampened our spirits, and frustration could be seen on most of the players' faces. Missed opportunities, poor tackling, and too many turnovers contributed to a miserable exhibition and a fourteen-point deficit. At halftime, the players lethargically jogged to the locker room. This was out of character. It appeared that they had already accepted defeat. Some of the players went through the motions of bravado and pseudo-enthusiasm. But it seemed to be superficial. We, as coaches, made our adjustments and gave intense and fiery speeches. We hoped that the second half would bring about a reversal of play. But you could feel it in the air. For some reasons, these warriors did not believe that they could overcome the odds.

Suddenly and much to our surprise, Kyle raised his hand and made a request to speak to the team. We gave him the floor. There was a period of long silence as he looked into the eyes of each player. He quietly, yet with conviction and strength, said the following, "I have worked with all of you and fought against odds in the trenches. You are not only my teammates, but also my family. We have worked hard to improve, and I will proudly stand by all of you. But the time has come for us to raise our level. This sloppy and weak play is a thing of the past." After a few more seconds of silence, he pointedly added, "Play from your heart. Reach down inside of yourself and give it 100 percent. Play for yourself and your family." There seemed to be some inner soul-searching by all members of the team. Suddenly a fellow teammate broke the silence. "You heard what he said, let's do it." The players charged out of the locker room with renewed heart and determination. The quiet yet powerful speech was the ignition we needed to launch us to victory. It was offered from the heart by a young man of few words and yet so much to say and give.

The following week, Kyle was two minutes late to practice. He knew our policy concerning tardiness. After practice, he went to the "hill" to run. The hill was twenty yards long and had a very steep grade. Each player was to run three hills for each minute they were late. Two minutes late means a player should run six hills. That should take about five to seven minutes to run. After nearly twenty minutes, I went over to the hill to check on him. He was at the bottom of the hill with hands on his knees and staring at the ground. He was straining to regain his breath. "How many have you run?" I inquired. "I don't know, probably fifteen or so," he replied. "You only have to run six," I exclaimed. "Not if I am supposed to be a leader," he gasped. I do not know how many he ran. But when he returned to the locker room, it looked as if he had been in a war. He must have run well over thirty.

During the next day in casual conversation, I inquired about the tardiness. I mean this warrior was always the first to arrive at and the last to leave practice. "I am curious, why were you late?" I asked. He looked me straight in the eye and said, "I was helping a new freshman player with his pads." "He has never played before and had a difficult time with them" he added. "Kyle, you have got to be kidding. It is commendable to help a new and probably uncertain prospective player. Next time, let me know. We do not want to give consequences far beyond expectations. You were providing a service for the team. It shows an unselfish responsibility to act as you did," I explained. He nodded in agreement but added a subtle reply, "No excuses, I always need to be on time," he said. I assume that he felt he needed to go far beyond expectations if he were to assume the role of leadership. My heart welled with pride when I thought back of how much this individual unknowingly had given to this team.

The season ended strong, and the players felt a high level of pride because of their effort and noticeable improvement. All of the coaches look back at that quiet speech as being the turning point in the season.

The year was coming to an end. It was the end of May, and I was combing the progress reports to check up on all of the young people in our football program. Being in an academic-oriented community, almost all of our young people had grades higher than Cs. I ran across three or four players that had Ds and quickly jotted their names down. I was coming to the end of the alphabet and, much to my chagrin, ran across a name that put me in shock. There was Kyle's name with two Fs.

Now, I had Kyle as a student the previous year, and he was carrying a 3.6 grade point average. I knew he was responsible, intelligent, and disciplined. There had to be some error or mistake. I went to the teachers and asked about his performance. Much to my surprise, both teachers said that during the past six weeks, he had done nothing, and his normally high test scores were plummeting. "I can't put my finger on it, he just seems different. He seems apathetic and uninterested in learning. It is just not the same Kyle," one of the teachers stated.

The very next day I called him to my room to discuss his grades. I expressed concern and even shock about his marked decrease in grade status. His response demonstrated respectful assurance. "I admit I have been slacking, but I guarantee that the grades will come up," he stated. And his prediction was correct. He made up the work and aced the finals to give him Cs in both classes. Little did I know that there was far more to this change that I had imagined. I had just hit the tip of the iceberg. There was so much more below the surface that I had totally overlooked.

I had noted that Kyle was not attending the "optional" workouts in the summer. He was also missing the weight training sessions. I asked his buddies about his absence, and they had or did not give an answer. One of his friends suggested that he may be spending time with his grandfather in another state. This seemed plausible, but unlikely. I called him at home and left messages with his sister. But I received no response. It was so unlike him to just drop from the scene.

About a week before doubles began, Kyle wandered into the weight room. He looked sheepishly in my direction as he checked the workout schedule. I went over to him and matter-of-factly stated that we had missed him during the summer. He apologized and said that he was gone all summer, but did continue to work out. He looked thinner, but just as strong and defined. He finished his workout and assured me that he would be present the next day. But I was uncertain about what to think. I mean, he had always been straight with me and yet I was confused about the ambiguity of his answers and actions.

I locked up the weight room and was headed toward my car when I spotted Kyle sitting on the hill a few feet away. He slowly got up and approached me. He seemed hesitant and almost embarrassed. He looked down and began to mumble the following, "Coach, I have been gone all summer. But I have been in rehab. My drug addiction was getting out of hand, and I was afraid that it not only could completely consume me, but change my relationship with all of the people I care about," he stated. There was a long period of silence, and my mouth must have dropped from surprise. I always felt I could detect these problems and was perceptive about behavioral changes. I prided myself in knowing student and student-athletes as people—not just members of an organization. But I missed the boat on this one. "Kyle, I had no idea," I exclaimed. "Yeah, even my best friends and mother had not an idea either," he answered. "I guess being an introvert and blending in with the crowd worked, and I was able to pull it off for some time," he added.

We must have sat for over an hour and talked about his addiction, rationale, and overall perspectives. I guess

I knew the student, football player, and the person who suited up and went home after practices. I did not know the inner workings and feelings of this complex individual. Since his graduation, we have met a number of times. Now we talk about him as a complete person. Incidentally, we had a great season the next year. Of course it was led by the heart and character of Kyle. And more importantly, he has been drug free for over twenty years and continues to have an impact on those around him.

EVEN GOOD LEADERS MAY WIN

As a person, Derrick was a parent's and an educator's dream. He was honest, respectful, interesting, and positive. However, to rebellious young teens or hypocritical media, this person would be labeled as a nerd or geek. What is so tragic is that these people, oftentimes, face more social ridicule and sarcasm than that of the rebellious or negative person.

Derrick was a person who possessed diverse interests and talents. His knowledge spanned over a wide range of subjects. He was never afraid to challenge himself to learn more about a given subject. What was even more unique, he did not have to excel or have experienced a given subject to become involved or interested. In other words, he would not have to play basketball or the violin, to demonstrate a genuine interest in sports or music. The ability to show interest despite ones inclinations and talents is a rare characteristic that is noted in only a few individuals.

Derrick had almost all of the ingredients necessary for effective leadership. He had an excellent speaking voice that projected well and attracted listeners. He also had command of language and used jargon or expression that would interest all audiences. He liked and communicated openly with both students and faculty. His interest in human diversity would certainly endear him to a wide variety of individuals. He was well organized, clever, objective, and responsible. He could read a problem, suggest a solution, and identify people who could work effectively together. In short, he had almost every characteristic necessary for successful leadership.

Derrick certainly wanted a leadership role. He told me that he had run for various class or school offices since the first grade. He laughed with guarded pain when he candidly stated, "I believe that my record is 0-15." Yet he had enough personal resilience to climb his way back up to the campaign trail every year. But I'm sure he was hiding the deep disappointment and pain from his exercise in futility.

In his sophomore year, he developed one of the most creative and ingenious campaigns I have ever witnessed. It identified and offered solutions to problems in a catchy and creative way. The humorous slogans and catch phrases had students and faculty talking and offering the highest of all compliments—imitation. Unfortunately, I believe that much of the time it was ridiculing rather the flattery. I had to remind myself constantly that Derrick had some very "weak" flaws for becoming elected—honesty, sincerity, organization, creativity, morals, and ethics. In many social circles, these traits are labeled as corny or old-fashioned. It is so tragic and superficial. As one might predict, he lost again to make his record 0-16.

A week later, we were talking before school. I could tell by his body language and roving eyes that there was something serious on his mind. He certainly was not his gregarious and enthusiastic self. He was hesitant and appeared to be feeling for words. He eventually sputtered out, "I have had enough frustration with my political flops." Tears clouded his eyes as he added, "I really do not know if I can take this anymore. I do not want to change my ideals, ethics, or goals. Yet if I do not 'play the game,' I feel that I will be faced with more frustration. I am tired of ill-prepared, unimaginative, and vulgar candidates winning." He added, "Gutter jokes and slimy roles seem to be ingredients for success." He wondered if he should change his area of competition. Maybe he should leave the political arena.

Derrick had expressed frustration over not being a part of the "in" or "popular" crowd. "I know that there are few people, who have the ability to lead effectively in this school," he expressed. "But even the strongest of us have our breaking point," he added. "Derrick, you have answered your own question," I said. "Because you do have these qualities, you cannot fulfill your own goals or destiny by incorporating the term *hang it up*," I added. He peered up through his glasses and quietly nodded and said, "I guess I just needed somebody else to validate what I felt was necessary anyway." The discussion never came up again.

The next year our school was facing a very serious crisis. The school board had received pressure from parents across town, whose children had attended other schools, to close our school. They had argued that since two schools were closed on one side of town, one should be closed on the other. The need for strong and effective leadership now reached the level of crisis. Peers now looked for a powerful and effective leader. The dirty infantile slogans lost much of their luster. Students now knew that the leadership of the school was not just in name. The leadership role was not just symbolic; it impacted the future of all students. They now turned to Derrick. He was elected student body president in a landslide victory. As expected, Derrick rolled up his sleeves and went to work. He organized committees, arranged discussions with principals and public officials, and facilitated protest projects. His tireless effort left a lasting impact with the school board. They had decided to not close our school. The students were relieved to know that this battle had turned. But the relief and excitement was short-lived. Unfortunately, the school board held a secret session during the summer and reversed their decision.

Much to our frustration, we were to merge with our rival school. The feeling between the schools was not one of pleasantry. Leadership now was more critical than before. For the second time, the cute clichés and vulgar actions of past comedians held little amusement or attraction to our student body. The time had arrived when effective and mature leadership was vital. Now the personality characteristics exemplified by Derrick became applicable, if not necessary.

Teachers and students felt betrayed by the school board and were hostile about being forced to merge with our rival. The other school had similar, but less hostile, feelings. The merged school decided to have two student body presidents to bridge the gap and make the transition easier. The year began with suspicion, segregation, and uncertainty for the merged student body. The two student body presidents worked hard to unite the students. Finally, during a talent assembly, some of the barriers were broken. Derrick had orchestrated a lip-sync performance. Numerous humorous and talented acts captivated the interest of the diverse student body. Derrick and his partner finally rolled on stage to lip-sync two of the songs performed by the Blues Brothers. His showmanship and animated actions brought a standing ovation. People in the audience were "high-fiving," smiling, and truly enjoying themselves. Many teachers expressed their feelings about the assembly and corresponding enthusiasm. Apparently, the school had never seen such a display of positive feelings and attitudes.

Multicultural, pep, and student-need assemblies were greeted with a new sense of loyalty and enthusiasm. Forums and free exchange of ideas were encouraged among all of the students. People received status and recognition for diverse interests and talents. Our leader reached out to all people in the school and was greeted with the respect and enthusiasm he so justly deserved. This school had received a solid foundation for growth spearheaded by a versatile, mature, and positive young man. In all of my years in education, I have never witnessed a student body officer have such a large impact on a school and all of its students.

As one might expect, Derrick has ventured into many diverse occupations and interests since graduating from college. In each situation I am sure he leaves a positive feeling for all involved. Oh, and one conclusive remark might show an interesting parallel. There was another leader who had a similar win-loss record to that of Derrick. His name—Abe Lincoln.

The Power to Overcome the Odds

Darren's class was talented and highly motivated. When they entered the school as ninth graders, teachers and coaches expressed excited anticipation for the ensuing four years. In a school where academic and athletic excellence was rare, there was hope that this class may help establish strong leadership and new traditions. In four years, our perceptions were verified through graduation and college entrances.

Of course, like most groups, the road to accomplishment was filled with challenges and pitfalls. Each individual would choose their own route or method to navigate over or around the obstacles. While a few sailed through with only small bumps in the road, others faced trials and tribulations so large that only a few people can accurately identify with the heavy burdens. It seemed almost miraculous that these tough knocks only strengthened these young people, and they repeatedly picked themselves off the ground to reach and attain near unimaginable goals.

The numerous successful examples seemed to be beacons of hope for the young people that would follow. Although a few stumbled and fell along the way, most fought through the adversity to reach a high level of achievement. The twists and turns just seemed to be a greater opportunity to overcome adversity and accomplish feats that raised eyebrows throughout the city.

Darren faced odds rare and formidable. These obstacles were not exclusive, and most other people would collapse under the burden of this heavy load. He had been abandoned by both parents. Dad resided in a controlled environment funded by the state. Mom walked the streets searching for clients. On one occasion, while driving down the street that led to his house and neighborhood, he hesitantly and yet matter-of-factly pointed her out on the corner while attempting to drum up business. His embarrassment was obvious as he quietly uttered, "I talk to her about once a year." After a period of silence, I simply replied, "I'm sorry . . ." as my voice trailed off. "It has got to be tough," I added. "It's just the way it is," he retorted. "But I have my grandma and sister," he said as he blankly stared out the window.

I had been to his house a number of times. His sister appeared to be a "typical" ten-year-old. Grandma was a lady who possessed and expressed a high standard of morals. However, numerous physical ailments kept her housebound. A failing heart, high blood pressure, gout, and severe joint problems made mobility next to impossible. Yet she did her utmost to hold them together as a family. A crack house operated next door to him, and the "Crips Gang" spent all hours of the day and night across the street or within the immediate vicinity. There were numerous times that he was "approached" by gang members in hope of converting him to their cause. This would be followed with phone or direct threats. But he fought temptation to join any of the "families" and stayed focused on academic and athletic goals.

Unfortunately, his academic goals seemed secondary in nature and were primarily reached to ensure athletic participation. And he certainly could perform in the athletic arena. He was a solid basketball player but had the skill and love for football. Despite his chunky appearance, he was quick off the ball and very agile. Playing the interior, he was, oftentimes, outsized but rarely outplayed. Even as a sophomore, he was able to hold his own against older, more experienced and larger players.

We were a solid team his sophomore year and all returning players looked forward to the following season. Extensive time and effort in the off-season conditioning and weights, mixed with talent and intensity looked like a great formula for success. Practices were positive and intense, with a "seasoning" of humor and harmless pranks. Our smaller senior class was a mixed bag of experienced and first-year players. The success we had experienced on my first two seasons was new, and first-year players were anxious to participate. It was surprising to note their adaptability and success on this new field of play.

Labor Day was just a few practices away when we ran into a few bumps on the road. Three of our players sustained injuries that made position adjustment necessary. The injuries would probably keep them out of games for two to five weeks. But we had sufficient "cannon fodder" to weather the storm. Our jamboree on the holiday weekend was a success, and we felt confident going into our first game.

The players were given time off through most of the weekend. We scheduled a light workout Monday evening in helmets, shorts, shirts, and shoes. I felt it mandatory to help the players refocus on football and the following week. But much to my surprise, three of our key players were missing. They were starters, and I hoped they had legitimate excuses.

Unfortunately, I had serious doubts. Darren happened to be one of the three. In our program, no matter what the excuse, any player who missed practice would be relegated to our scouting squad the next practice. Our rules stated that if there was a validated excuse, a person could play in the game and even start if they ran their laps and outworked their teammates. However, if the absence was unexcused, they would have to run thirty laps and could not play in the following game.

Prior to practice on Tuesday, I brought the three into the coaches' office to inquire about the absences. They really did not need to answer. Their faces were "neon signs" of guilt. They knew they would miss the first game and still have to run their laps and aid in game preparation by excelling on the scouting squad. They met and exceeded expectations by making it a challenge in drills and scrimmages. Unfortunately, our worst nightmares materialized. Jim, one of the best strikers I have ever coached dislocated his shoulder and was out for the season. Darren tore his ACL and lateral ligaments. He, too, was incapacitated for the season. And one of our key defensive backs lasted three weeks before he went down. It started an epidemic of injuries that can only be conjured up in somebody's worst nightmares.

Darren did not have any money or insurance. My help would be miniscule in comparison to the overall cost. Fortunately, my doctor, who is one of the most caring individuals I have known, agreed to perform surgery "pro bono." The operation was a success, and now he was in for a long period of rehab. Unfortunately, his physical therapy would have to be administered after office hours. He was able to enter the facility through the back door, and one of the therapists, would stay and help with the rehab process. Another serious roadblock had been thrown in his path, but with perseverance, Darren was able to overcome the pain and discomfort to conquer another adverse situation.

As expected, through gritty and hard work, he put his body through the necessary discipline and painful rehabilitation to return to his previous form. He built himself to an even higher level and certainly was primed to help lead his team to a championship the following season.

And what a fantastic season it was. Newspapers, television, and radio stations dedicated time to cover the phenomenal climb to the pinnacle or highest level of the league. A one-point victory started the season, and except for one loss, the season was fabulous and brought home the trophy. Darren was among the fine group of seniors that were leaders in so many different ways. However, unexpected obstacles would again challenge the strongest of individuals.

About midway through the season, I was on the field working with our punters and kickers after practice. I heard some commotion coming from the direction of the locker room. I could see arms from a couple of my players motioning in my direction. As I started to walk to the locker room, I could only guess what all of the hubbub was about. My mind was racing with visions of an injured player who had slipped or stumbled as he entered the locker room. By then one of my players met me and exclaimed, "Coach, there is going to be a fight, you gotta hurry." *A fight*, I wondered as I ran down the stairs. Who and why, I asked myself. There was a lot of screaming coming from the main locker and shower area. There among the team were "outsiders" yelling obscenities and making wild accusations. I knew the leader and pulled him aside. Anger and panic were written all over his strained face. "Tommy, think about what you are saying," I firmly stated. "You are on probation, and any conflict you instigate or become involved in will only lead to trouble for you and your buddies. Secondly, this is a closed locker room to the outside public or students," I firmly stated. I quietly escorted him outside while trying to calm the unexplainable turmoil being stirred up. His buddies followed. As he began to leave the campus, he looked at me and said, "No offense to you, Coach, but this is not over." *Not over,* I asked myself. *What is not over?*

Two minutes later, Darren came charging out of the locker room screaming obscenities, with Jim close on his hills. "What is this all about?" I inquired. "Tommy is right!" Darren yelled as he walked toward the driveway. Suddenly Jim interrupted by emphatically saying, "Darren, you know that that is a bunch of garbage. All they want to do is rain on our parade because they are jealous and know that they are going nowhere," he added. Darren glared at Jim and verbally scolded him for being a sell-out. "Darren, you want to destroy our family because of a few stupid remarks made by people who have no idea about our team, the game, and the school. They are the prejudice ones that are selling out our race," Jim stated. There was a brief period of silence as they exchanged stares. I just could not believe what I was hearing. These two best friends were almost to the point of blows over what. Darren was still yelling at Jim as he walked off the campus.

"What the heck is going on?" I asked Jim. "Oh, Tommy is some phony gang leader supposedly. He was in our locker room making accusations about prejudice and racial discrimination. Coach, this is a bunch of garbage. We have worked too long and hard to have some outsiders ruin it all," Jim angrily stated. "Nobody else has any idea what they are talking about. The only ones that have gotten stirred up are Darren and Mike," he added. His face reflected disappointment, confusion, and anger. He gave a deep sigh before he said, "I'll call Darren tonight and see if I can't get it straightened out." "Jim, *you* call me tonight, and let me know what happens," I commanded. We then sat and talked for quite awhile. I gave him a ride home, and he assured me he would call as soon as he communicated with Darren.

It was about 11:00 PM when I received a call from Jim. "Coach, you better give Darren a call. I got nowhere. It was like talking to a wall," he said. I agreed to call Darren. Unfortunately, all I received were recordings five different times. I worried that I may not have opportunity to communicate with him before the next day. Finally, about 2:30 AM, he called me back. He was irrational and talking without listening. This was not the Darren I knew. Sometimes he had a short fuse but would calm himself and open his mind. We could freely exchange thoughts and ideas. But this was different. He was spouting off about that it was all coming down tomorrow. When I inquired about the meaning, Darren would just repeat or rephrase his statement. After my repeated efforts to get a word in edgewise, he abruptly hung up the phone. My return calls were to no avail. Finally, about 4:15 AM he called back. He informed me that nothing was going to happen to me or Mr. Thomas, who was a very popular principal. "Coach, about fifteen guys are coming to school tomorrow with justice in mind. We are going to shoot all those blank, blank bigots. You and Mr. Thomas will be left alone. But everyone else is fair game," he angrily stated. I'm sure he could hear the frustration in my voice when I replied, "Darren, you know that Mr. Thomas and I will do everything in our power to stop you." I added, "You'll have to go through us." "If we have to hold you down, we will," he quickly retorted. He then informed me that if the cops

100

were there, it would just happen another day. We bantered back and forth for another forty-five minutes. Exhausted, I told him to listen to my final statement. "Darren, I care about you too much to see you throw everything away for the team and yourself. Anybody that would try to wreck all you and this team have accomplished cares nothing about principle, people, or ideals. They just want to take people of their own race and destroy all of their hopes and dreams. Not from a point of justice, but rather hatred, jealousy, and bigotry," I firmly stated. "And I have one question to ask you. Would you do what Tommy is doing to somebody you cared about? Would you do this to any of your family?" I added. There was a period of silence before I hung up.

I quickly called Mr. Thomas. He told me that he and I would be there early in the morning to address and hopefully stop this nightmare. Darren had implied that it was going down in the morning. Mr. Thomas had alerted the police, and they would be primed for our call if needed. About ten minutes before first period was to begin, we saw three cars pull up to the far corner of the building. I recognized one of the cars because of the symbols painted on the side. Quickly, we started to walk toward the cars. Suddenly, we saw somebody in a hooded shirt run up to the window of the first car. He was pointing his finger and yelling. We quickened our pace. When we got about twenty-five yards away, the three cars sped off. I was pleasingly surprised to see that the hooded figure was Darren. He looked at us, and in a quiet yet stern voice, said, "Sorry, that will never happen again." He then walked away without saying anything else. This was a serious issue that needed to be addressed. I am sure that Mr. Thomas had Darren in his office later that day to discuss the series of events.

Darren and Jim were the first ones ready for our meeting before practice. We did not address each other about the subject. Even though there seemed to be a stiffness in the air, the team did a good job of trying to focus on what was at hand. And Darren and Jim had solid practices. But needless to say, there was still an uneasiness on the field. I wondered about how long it would take to bring this team back as a family. Darren must have sensed the necessity to bring this unity back because at the end of practice, he asked to address the team. "I promise to never let some outsider get in the way of our family and its goals again," he stated. He added a few more sentences. The message was strong and to the point. The team showed guarded approval of Darren and what he had said. But the healing had begun, and unity was quickly restored. After practice, I brought Darren into the office to talk. We talked for over an hour about the problem. We spoke openly about adversity and how other people wanted to see us fail. But it wasn't until after the season was over that we talked more specifically about the series of events. At that time, Darren informed me that the gang members had just about every type of gun you could imagine. The problem could have mushroomed into one of the biggest disasters in our country's history. Darren had stopped one of the most dangerous situations imaginable from happening. He never spoke about the subject again to me or as far as I know to anyone else. The situation was nothing to brag or discuss openly. Yet, I am sure that Jim made it known to others about what a heroic and proper action Darren had taken. True to form, Jim did not talk about his own contribution.

The season was rewarding to say the least. Media coverage helped the whole community realize what a great feat these young men had accomplished. Our team and individual players received numerous awards. Our team members were leaders of a parade, spoke at banquets, and received some of the most prestigious awards. Two of our players were chosen to participate in the state game. This was one of the few times that players from the high school were to be represented in the summer showcase.

I was also honored by being given the opportunity to assist in coaching duties. Throughout my coaching tenure, I have had opportunity to coach a number of all-star teams. I have been amazed at how quickly young people bond and become a unified group or team.

During the week of practice prior to the game, one of our school's rep Carl found it easy to bond quickly with all of all-star players throughout the state. He was gregarious and open to diverse individuals. Darren, on the other hand, was a little slower to identify with all members of the teams. However, his quick wit and humorous actions became a powerful draw, and his popularity skyrocketed. Both Darren and Carl became defensive starters and played at a high level. Because the team bonded quickly and possessed obvious talent, success seemed inevitable.

The opposing team practiced on the same fields. Team members from both teams became acquainted and close. Yet when the game approached, you could see the intensity and competitive levels increase. The people who manage the week and game did an excellent job of integrating cooperation and competition.

There were three other players who were honored from our league. Like Darren, they were of minority status. One was a defensive lineman, Andre, who would line up right next to Darren. He was a talented yet a very insecure individual. Unfortunately, he wore his emotions on his sleeve and would lose his cool frequently. As coaches, we worked very hard to help him deal with his high anxiety and uncontrolled anger. Darren played a large role in working with Andre to better play under control and with a selfless attitude. We were pretty excited about the upcoming game, and it seemed that all of the pieces were falling into place.

The day of the game came very quickly. The opposing teams, who had eaten, played together, and grew close as friends had prepared to the best of their abilities. It is a curious irony that closest friends or relatives increase their level when competing against each other. The hitting and intensity level was very high prior to the game. This was noted on the opening kickoff as players crashed into each other at inspirationally high velocity. That intensity level even increased throughout the game. As the teams battled back and forth, we could see the temperature level rising. Competition and sportsmanship seemed perfectly balanced until Andre got blocked from behind. It was totally legal because it occurred in the box. And accordingly, there was no flag on the play. Unfortunately, Andre completely lost his poise, and a week of cooperative education appeared to be flushed. He directed expletive words at the ref. He then spit in his direction. He was immediately thrown out of the game. I had to go on the field and forcibly bring him back to the bench. I commanded him to sit on the bench and not move. I was angered, appalled, and deeply embarrassed for the team, coaches, and Andre. As I walked away, I will never forget what I heard next. Darren approached Andre and said, "You shamed our team. You shamed your school. But mostly you shamed our race and yourself." He then walked away without adding another word. His brief statements probably did more to solidify the messages directed to Andre over the past week than anything a coach or administrator could say.

Darren had again left an impact on the life of a fellow student and teammate. He had helped somebody else overcome their obstacles. And amazingly after the game, Andre apologized to the team and thanked Darren and the coachers for their help. Darren has faced numerous other obstacles. He has stumbled and fallen yet, like always, eventually righted himself so that he could move forward.

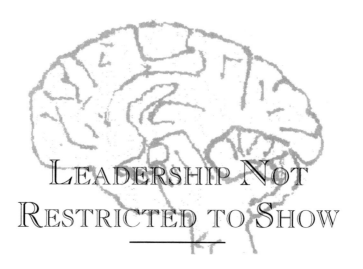

Leadership Not Restricted to Show

Effective leadership depends on numerous variables. Group chemistry, a common cause, mutual goals, and a necessity for fulfilled roles are just a few of the factors that can determine success or obscurity. One of the most significant factors is a high regard and respect directed to the leader by the group members.

Lena did not possess many of the overt or easily identifiable characteristics of leadership. Initially, her leadership skills were not fully appreciated by fellow team members or coaches. Yet, as a sophomore, I noted numerous outstanding personal and athletic characteristics. She had excellent hand-eye coordination, superior intelligence, and an excellent work ethic. Although a "wisp" of a girl, she possessed a soft, shooting touch and good feet. She moved very quickly for a girl of five feet ten inches. She was not egotistical or even a demonstration of confidence. She would communicate in a genuine and soft manner with all of the players on the team. Yet her unselfish and group attitude seemed to be a solid foundation for leadership.

Lena and her fellow team members were talented, competitive, and highly motivated. They all put in endless extra hours to hone their basketball skills. They proved their talent and worth by winning numerous tournaments and championships. During the off-season, many of them would work on ball handling, shooting, and footwork drills seven or eight times a week. Lena would practice as much as her busy schedule would permit. While she demonstrated steady improvement, most of her teammates improved in "leaps in bounds." Within a year, it was evident that they had passed her by.

This was a difficult time for her. "Coach, you know I have been trying to work hard on my skills, but I have very little extra time. Almost all of my free time is devoted to practice," Lena said. "It is not that I believe I should be playing more, it is just that I do not want you or the rest of the team to think that I am sluffing," she added. All I could ask her to do was give as much as her schedule would allow.

Most of the time, when young people see others surpassing them, they find a reason to avoid competing or turning out for the team. But, this was not the case with Lena. She stayed strong and poised even as she saw the gap widening between her and most of the other players. She maintained an inner strength and demonstrated a mature and unselfish attitude. Her playing time averaged just over six minutes a game. In the meantime, the team continued to improve, and the winning streak was growing.

As a senior, her playing time decreased even further. Her spirits never were darkened. Her enthusiasm increased, and her role as a leader left a large impact on the team. Stress increased as the competition took turns at trying to break the win streak. Her stable influence and true leadership became critical. Her unflappable and solid image was truly a beacon of strength for all of the team members.

One of the most important traits or qualities of a leader is earned respect. For any young person, this is very hard to establish and maintain. Generally, the visible and noted qualities of talent and recognition seem to be the most successful in helping a person gain respect. In cases where dominance or success is not obvious, peers will pay tribute by giving a less talented person a superficial reward or condescending pat on the back. Although people have good intentions, their reward can be considered insulting or demeaning. However, Lena's role was offered out of respect and necessity.

Lena was chosen team captain by a unanimous vote. The effectiveness of her leadership never diminished because of decreased playing time. Athletes respected her because of who she was and what she symbolized. It is tough to remain loyal when the role you are playing is less visible and more indirect. She understood her shortcomings and stressed the importance of team unity with objective remarks, praise, and enthusiasm. I also have admiration for the other team members who saw past the "glitz" of newspaper articles and physical talent. Today, I am sure that Lena will never know how much she contributed to the success of these teams, but her teammates and I will.

ARE YOU STILL MOCKING ME FROM BEHIND?

It was a typical classroom of cultural and social diversity. And the extremes tipped both ends of the spectrum. Six of the students in the class did everything they could to become associated with the "counterculture." These images were important for social identification and recognition.

They projected a mixed image of indifference and rebellion. They would use drab apparel and various nonverbal messages to sell the image. For instance, instead of walking, they would swagger or slog (drag slowly). They also would send nonverbal messages through the infamous eye roll, folded arms, or eye avoidance. These body messages, along with deep sighs or groans, expressed the disdain for the class, school, and education in general. After sitting down, they would slouch and push their desk away in disgust. Their sloppy, unkempt, and dreary clothes further reinforced a desired image. Apathy had become the largest piece of armor used by the group for emotional protection. Like most rebellious people, this projected image of rebellion was more likely a covering or protection against the pain of failure. Or maybe it was just a ploy for attention or peer recognition.

The group members all went through various degrees of change throughout the year. Three of them began to change and eventually became solid students by the end of the school year. Two others lasted most of the year but eventually withdrew from school. But Sol has a completely different story. He had always demonstrated a high degree of intelligence and a genuine desire to learn. He was liked and respected by all members of the clique. Despite his appearance, eventually the whole class learned to appreciate his ability and would defer to his knowledge.

Although he continued to maintain a close relationship with his friends, he began to associate with diverse people. Despite the fact that he had begun to expand his social world, he never lost a special feeling and understanding of the outcastes. But this empathy did not keep him from choosing a different path. He began to excel in the classroom. His grades changed from Bs and Cs to As. He became an academic leader in the school. It seemed as if he now had realized his potential and could see that the recognition and status were worth the effort.

Sol truly was a delight to have in class. He spearheaded discussions and debates and would act as a group facilitator for activities and projects. It was evident that he was instrumental in helping almost all of the students in the class raise their level of performance.

As the school year was winding down, Sol came up to me and asked if I thought it was too late for him to try to play football. He already had a number of strikes against him. First of all, he would be a junior the following year. Secondly, he had never participated in sports. And finally, he was overweight, soft, and out of shape. "I know that I have a long way to go, Coach, but I want to give it a shot," he said pleadingly. "Sol, any person can turn out, but it takes a unique person to stick with an uphill challenge,"

I replied. "Coach, I will do whatever is necessary for me to have some success. I do not expect to be a star, I just want to contribute," he added. As a coach, I have always believed that athletics is for all people; no matter how much talent or experience they exhibit. When athletic participation is only reserved for the elite or gifted, it has become exclusive and should be removed from public education. Even though I feel we should never discourage a young person, coaches should be careful to not put people into positions where the activity destroys a self-image.

I told Sol that I did not want this to be a negative experience. One of the worst things that could happen is that you quit feeling you are a failure. Despite the uncertainty, Sol decided to commit himself to hard work in the weight room until football started in August. He then would give football a chance.

We were running an after-school weight program that was open to all individuals. Like clockwork, Sol was there every day, putting himself through the paces.

But before we started, we had to find out where he was in terms of strength. I knew he was out of shape but was surprised to see just how weak he was. Sol weighed over 250 pounds yet; he could not bench eighty-five or curl twenty pounds. He struggled with leg-extension drills and was breathing very heavy after the simplest workouts. However, he was able to leg press over three hundred pounds. This was probably attributed to the fact that he had to carry a large amount of weight just to move around.

Some of the students were curious about his workouts. They had never seen such a large person that was so weak and inept. We had been working out for about twenty minutes when one of the coaches stopped by before going up for basketball practice. He stared in amazement as Sol struggled to balance these lightweights. Later on in the coach's office, he quipped in a sarcastic tone, "You're trying to get extra points for working with charity cases." He added, "There is no hope. It is too little too late." Even though he may be right, I felt that the remarks were cheap and insulting to both of us.

Sol never knew about those cute little sarcastic remarks. However, he did know that many student-athletes knew about his intention and were sure that he had no chance. Despite the doubt and uncertainty, each day he showed improvement. Out of true grit, he raised his bench press to two hundred and curls to forty-five pounds. Other players would make remarks of disbelief about his change. They knew about the sacrifice and embarrassment he had to withstand to stay on task. It was obvious that he was gaining respect from others as well as himself.

Despite this success, Sol's biggest challenge still lay ahead. A first-time athlete was about to go through an uphill battle of daily double practice. Sol had prepared himself for exhausting and hard-nose practices. I had prepared Sol for frustration, confusion, and disappointment. "Sol, the real satisfaction and joy of the game will not begin until after a couple of games," I warned cautiously. "You will need to suffer through the conditioning and tough practices before you reap the reward," I added. I was secretly hoping that a real love and understanding of the game would follow. For the first three weeks, Sol did struggle. He was last in every conditioning drill. Because of his inexperience and poorly conditioned body, he was always picking himself off the ground during contact drills.

Sol was discouraged. His body language demonstrated frustration and depression. It was obvious that verbal positive reinforcement would only help to ease the pain temporarily. Even though all of his teammates were extremely positive and encouraged him every step of the way, this was primarily a battle that he would have to fight alone. Later he told me that he thought about quitting at least a dozen times. But something inside of him said that he would regret that for the rest of his life. (This is mature and powerful reasoning from a sixteen-year-old.)

Slowly Sol started to improve. Even though he was only playing eight to ten minutes a game at the JV level, he was gaining valuable experience. His size had helped gain minimal success. In third or fourth down and short situations, they could follow Sol for the necessary yardage. By the end of the season, he was playing almost a half.

But the varsity level would be a different story. Sol continued lifting weights all year. He lost a little weight but basically maintained the same body-build. Many people were amazed that this person, who used to be weak and insecure, had become so strong and confident. His body language now demonstrated poise, strength, and confidence.

With his first game of varsity on the horizon, he became anxious and uncertain. In the first game he participated in three plays. His play was uneventful. This token playing continued for another three games. His contribution on the field was minimal. However, he kept his intensity and supported the team emotionally and mentally. An injury left us with a hole in the defensive line rotation. A few of the coaches still had a preconceived idea of Sol and were reluctant to utilize his ability and strength.

However, another injury put our backs against the wall. Sol began to play over a quarter a game. By the seventh game, he was a starter and by the eighth game he became a force. He was unanimously chosen Most Improved and received the coveted Coaches' Award. At the end of the season, Sol said, "Coach, this is the greatest and most rewarding experience I have ever had. I love this game." But he gave us much more than he received. I do not believe Sol will ever know how much he inspired the coaches and his fellow team members.

Sol is now working and going to college. He certainly will tackle new challenges and break barriers to reach high levels of success. The dogged determination he used to become successful in the classroom and on the field will carry him a long ways.

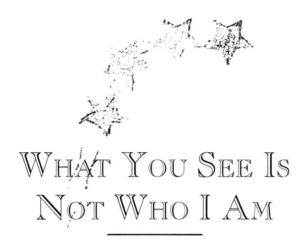

WHAT YOU SEE IS NOT WHO I AM

People demonstrate attitudes and emotions in a wide variety of ways. Oral expression can be a reflection of thoughts and overall personality. Yet the expression can easily become a cover-up. Even though it can bring about desired results and can con people in all walks of life, it truly is deceptive and is demonstration of character flaws. For example, people can falsely express love, caring, enthusiasm, appreciation, and honesty with vocabulary that is offered for devious and selfish reasons. The opposite can also occur. People express anger and pain in hopes of receiving positive feedback. There is no doubt that the "art" of the verbal con is often so polished that it is difficult to detect.

Generally a more honest expression of our attitude and personality is demonstrated through body language. Our facial expressions, eye contact, shoulder and trunk position, mobility, and overall presentation are much more difficult to cover up.

Teenagers seem to wear their attitudes on their shirtsleeves. They choose or do a poor job of covering up their emotions or feelings. There have been numerous times that students have asked me how I was able to read their minds. When, actually all that has occurred is the basic observance of body-language messages. Depression, distain cynicism, empathy, excitement are most honestly expressed by actions and not words.

Teachers become quite perceptive of general emotions and feelings. We can tell the overall attitude toward education and life in general by observing nonverbal language. I have found that not instituting a seating chart has opened opportunities to identify attitudes concerning education and overall respect. Students who have nixed education sit in the back of the room, have little or no school supplies, push their chairs away from their desk or the front of the room, and give little or defiant eye contact. Sighs, eye rolls, and constant clock-watching can also be telltale signs of apathy. Hopefully teachers can use this knowledge to help inspire less attentive students. On the other hand, students who place a higher value on education choose to sit near the front, maintain great eye contact, and sit straight and attentively. Even though the above mentioned are generalities, and there are numerous exceptions, most students follow the rules of this unwritten language.

On the first day of school, Susan entered the room, beautiful and dressed to the hilt. She did not choose to sit near the front, and as I watched her meander to the back of the room, I was reminded of the stereotypical "soshy snob." During the next week, many of my early presumptions seemed to be reinforced. Instead of taking notes during class discussion and lectures, she seemed aloof and appeared to be doodling in her notebook. If she did look up and make eye contact during class, it appeared as if she was skeptical and defiant about the subject matter or the class as a whole. To add to the assumed stereotypical perception, she acted indifferent and almost snooty to her classmates. It appeared that she felt superior to the teacher, fellow students, and even the class as a whole.

She did turn her homework in on time. It was organized and fairly well done. Maybe she just felt it necessary to jump through the academic hoops. I figured she would slide along in class and meet responsibilities solely for extrinsic reasons. But I wondered what would happen to her when she had to take a unit test about notes given in class and some basic readings.

We were preparing for our first unit test. Her almost-cynical looks typically spelled out "get me through this ordeal, so I can move on." On test day, she appeared bored and apathetic. Susan turned the test in sooner than most of the class. She went back to her seat and opened her notebook and appeared to be drawing creative additions to her doodles.

That night I was grading the tests. Upon coming across Susan's, I was shocked to say the least. Susan had aced the test with a score of 97 percent. Maybe she had foreknowledge of the subject before we began the unit of study. But I had some serious doubts. I handed back the tests with little fanfare other than a word of encouragement or a brief congratulation to students who had excelled.

When the bell rang, she slowly gathered her books and walked toward my desk and quietly said thanks. Why? I had no idea. Did she believe that I had given her a score that she did not deserve? About a week later, she offered another statement of appreciation. "For what?" I questioned "Just for the class and the information I have learned," she replied. "I guess I just love to learn," she added. I was taken aback to say the least. Was this a further con? Yet she seemed so sincere. Could I have misjudged her intentions and attitude in general?

As time went on, I learned there was much more depth to this young lady that I had overlooked. Her doodles were just additions to her notes and creative ways of encoding information. But her nonverbal communication was so defiant and indifferent. I soon began to realize that this talented and beautiful young lady was actually insecure and lacked confidence. Her surly exterior was protection from pain. Even though there was no logical explanation, it was evident that she had been shot down in some manner.

As the year progressed, she began to loosen up and offer impactic insight and comments to class discussions and debates. And she continued to reach the highest levels in all academic endeavors.

On one occasion we were talking after class. The subject matter dealt with her plans after graduation. She expressed uncertainty about what career she wanted to pursue. She was thinking about law or forensics. But money was a genuine concern. It seemed that she had to earn any money she spent on clothes or activities. We talked about applying for scholarships. Then the idea hit me. "Why not try out for the school's honorary court," I said. "If you were lucky enough to win, there are numerous scholarships available. The title of school princess would open numerous doors." I added. She was reluctant and expressed doubt in her ability to speak and answer impromptu questions. She also expressed concern about her lack of popularity. "There are so many girls who are going to try out," she said. They are so talented and popular, and I believe that inaccurate perceptions of me will inhibit any chance," she added. "So what," I said. "The experience will be great, and if you reach the finals, some doors will still be open. You have nothing to lose," I retorted. "Just embarrassment," she replied sheepishly. She finally agreed to think about the challenge.

After a few days of contemplation, she relented and decided to give it a try. There were over fifty girls who tried out to become the school's representative. All candidates were to offer speeches and impromptu responses to questions from a committee made up of dignitaries, city officials, and past winners. Her grace, poise, and intelligent responses impressed the committee, and she became a finalist. She now would compete in front of the entire student body.

The day before the assembly, she expressed extreme doubt and high anxiety. She was cordial and appeared more personal and friendly to her peers. But she avoided the "little game" of vote campaigning. Her insecurity was evident, but her demand for honesty and the avoidance of superficiality required her to play it straight and avoid politicking. She was determined to let her performance do her talking.

The next day at the morning assembly, six finalists gave presentations and offered impromptu answers. All of the candidates were excellent. There were a few slipups, but all in all each person performed well. Susan's performance was remarkable. She demonstrated poise, intelligence, and her speech was exquisite. After completion, the decision was to be made by the student body. Voting would take place in classes immediately after the assembly. The announcement of the winner would be made during a short assembly at the end of the day.

I felt Susan had a shot at winning. I had five of the candidates in my classes. Any person would be a good representative. But because of the adversity she faced, I quietly hoped for a victory for Susan. She, like the other candidates, had stress and high anxiety throughout the day. Finally, the announcement was made. Another girl had been chosen.

At the beginning of class the next day, this poised young lady walked to my desk and expressed appreciation for the encouragement she had received to participate in such a rewarding experience. But as she sat down at her desk, a young man who probably inaccurately thought of her as a snob, leaned over and said, "How does it feel to be a runner up?" Susan looked directly at him and said, "It hurts like heck." Surprised by her honesty and embarrassed, he sheepishly turned away and quietly took his seat. Unfortunately, I do not believe that he would ever realize or know about the quiet victory this previously insecure lady had earned. But, all in all, the contest itself was of lesser importance. What was important was the lessons both of us had learned. Susan learned that she had all of the ingredients for success and to never sell herself short. The increased confidence led to a successful college experience and a highly successful career as a lawyer. I learned that nothing is foolproof, and obvious assumptions should be avoided or at least guarded and an open mind maintained about all students.

RUGGEDLY SWEET AND STRAIGHT

She definitely could be called rough or rugged. And her mannerisms off and on the basketball court were similar. She would accept any challenge directed toward her with aggression and intensity. Her body language also expressed purpose and confidence. When she would look at a person, it was as if she was throwing up a warning sign of "dare not tread here." Her skeptical and aloof demeanor seemed to make fellow team members hesitant to extend their hand of friendship. A fifty-fifty mixture of respect and fear gave her an aura of power, yet a feeling of isolation. It was as if she was afraid to allow people to get too close to her for fear of personal pain or frustration. Descriptive adjectives, range from aggressive to sadistic, physical to mean, and intense to overbearing. But nobody would challenge her true grit and heart.

On the basketball court, she would play with reckless abandon. Yet there seemed to be a sense of cooperation and unselfish attitude that clashed with this abrasive personality. When Kacey was on the floor, bodies and balls would be flying all over the court. Yet there was a competitive goal that put purpose and balance into her play. Unfortunately, she would usually exit the court prematurely because of foul trouble. Her agile and quick hands could be overshadowed by this representation of power and assertiveness.

When Kacey played basketball, both teams would alter their style of play. Turnovers would double, and banged and bruised bodies became commonplace. Her speed and intensity would sometimes inhibit offensive balance and flow for both teams. This intense level of play would increase team and fan enthusiasm, and the energy level on the floor would skyrocket. As a coach, I would hold my breath in excited anticipation, knowing that the barometer in the room was jumping up a notch or two with each possession.

This conscientious attitude was infectious and quickly adopted and practiced by all members of the team. Her teammates respected her work ethic in practice and during the games. She could and would never give less than 100 percent in drills, conditioning, or play runs.

But it was not these qualities that stand out in my memory. It was her loyalty and understanding of human behavior that truly makes her special and unique. Beneath the rugged exterior, Kacey had a deep feeling and understanding of adversity, personal struggle, and needs.

Our youngest son had just arrived from Korea. Obviously, he was uncertain and scared about entering into a new world. Yet he was open to people who were taller, spoke differently, and possessed strange cultural practices and customs. All of the team members knew of this new addition to our family and were anxious to see and meet him.

We decided to take him to the gym during one of our "shootarounds." When he walked into the gym with his older brother, the much-anticipated meeting for the players quickly materialized. He was greeted with excitement and a genuine show of caring by almost all of the team members. Our young toddler was now an accepted part of the women's basketball team.

But as I looked at the curious demonstration of affection, I noticed that Kacey was missing. I saw her sitting at the end of the court with my eight-year-old son. She had the perception to know that it was the oldest who had more of an immediate need of security and acceptance. She understood how difficult it was for him to go from the center of attention to a "fringe player." This short-lived attention was instrumental in assuring him that his place in the program was still secure. To this day, I do not know if Kacey knows how much I appreciated her perception and deep understanding of human need.

Kacey was a varsity starter for three years. During that time she grew as a leader and endeared herself to all of the players in the program. She became a symbol of hard work, loyalty, and unselfishness. It was during Kacey's sophomore year that I was faced with one of the extremely low points of time in my thirty-two-year period of teaching and coaching.

The previous year, when Kacey was a ninth grader, we had shared in a very successful season. Although losing in the semifinals of the state tournament, we finished with a state best record of twenty-three and one. Unfortunately, the major, part of our team were seniors. This left a new challenge for the underclassmen to face. The younger players needed key leadership from our two main returning letter winners. It seemed that they had met the challenge and exceeded our expectations. They had led this young team to a successful summer season. However, one of the girls, who happened to be the leading scorer and dominant player, felt that the talent had left through graduation in the previous season. She felt that we were in for a year of frustration and struggle. She chose to leave the program for greener pastures and hopefully a championship pin. Although she moved in with another family to "legitimize" the defection, I could not help but feel that I had failed in providing her with the internal fortitude to see adversity as an opportunity to excel. The messages of loyalty, responsibility, and response to adversity are the cornerstones of what I believe to be the foundation for athletics. After this young lady left the program, my messages seemed empty and shallow. Obviously my words were not sufficient enough to bring out her leadership and feeling of responsibility.

The team floundered and struggled to regain or establish its own identity. The remaining senior starter worked hard to help players find their roles or niches. Eventually with the leadership of this senior and the intensity of Kacey, the team came together. The hard work and unity resulted in a very successful season and a trip to the state tournament. Kacey was a large part of this unsuspected success. Her pursuit of excellence and dogged determination help sweeten a bitter situation. Staying true to her tough, yet honest character helped mold a stable foundation for success.

On one occasion, Kacey happened to "run into" the girl who had left for greener pastures. Never afraid to express herself, she challenged the young lady. She expressed her displeasure in disloyalty, fear of responsibility, and lack of trust. She relayed the message to me as follows: "How could you run from your responsibility and ditch our family? I am disappointed with your cowardly act." She added, "I hope you don't run from your future families." The girl was speechless and taken aback by this pointed and principally directed message. As Kacey walked away, she turned and stated, "From now on, think about others before you act."

I was a bit taken aback by her strong verbal message. Yet Kacey stayed true to her beliefs and refused to ignore an injustice. Those were tough words of expectations coming from such a young person. And she lived up to those words. She never ignored her responsibility or turned her back on her team. She remained true to herself—tough on the outside with a genuine caring for others and an uncompromising belief in honor and justice.

Responsibility Need Not Be Boastful

One of the most serious problems facing our society today is the evolution or disintegration of the extended and nuclear family. In some cities, the saga of the unwed mother has reached epidemic proportions. Even the push in birth control education has made little impact on the growing social problem. It could be argued that the Pygmalion effect may occur, and our concerns and emphasis may facilitate the problem itself.

At our school, impregnated girls would receive status and attention from school officials and fellow students. Peers would offer empathy, support, curious attention, and superficial respect. School officials give necessary physical and psychological care or attention. What made the problem even more complex and confusing developed after the child was born. These girls would bring their "new toy" or child to school much to the joy of many peers. Other students would express delight, admiration, and, in many cases, envy these young girls. These girls, who oftentimes are without goals or hope, are suddenly the center of attention and delight in every opportunity to hold their child up like a trophy. In effect, they had become a desirable role model for other young girls.

It seems that we are in a "catch-22" dilemma. These young girls and their child need support and security from

126

peers and officials, yet this support reinforces and even promotes the problem we struggle to eliminate.

In class, we had been studying the change of the family structure over the past seventy-five years. We also had been examining the recent epidemic of teenage pregnancies. Many of the girls in the class expressed a genuine desire to acquire and maintain a sense of dignity and self-respect. They all felt that their children needed stability from a strong and unified family. They wanted to provide their children with a solid social, economical, and moral foundation. They felt a unified family would have a better chance to provide children with these emotional necessities.

A year later, Victoria came to talk with me after school. She had been a member of that class and spoken out strongly about moral and ethical standards. She had been a key contributor in class discussions and group research. When she entered the room, I noted she was pensive and contemplative. With a shaky and uncertain voice, she began to unravel a serious dilemma. She had just found out that she was pregnant. She expressed embarrassment and confusion. She said, "I feel so hypocritical. I also feel that I have let you, the class, and myself down." We further discussed her feelings and emotions to a semi-state of resolve. It seemed that she had overcome the obsession with guilt and began to focus on solutions.

The father was her immature and irresponsible boyfriend. She did not feel that he could or would accept any ownership of the problem. "I know that he is legally responsible for the child, but I feel that he himself is emotionally a child. I hoped we could meet this problem as a team. However, I now know that I must rely on myself for the benefit of the child," she stated. Even though we spent a long time discussing the pros and cons of abortion, it was quite evident that she intended to have the child. "That would be a violation of my morals and ethics. Just because I have made one mistake does not mean that I should make another," she continued. I came to realize that she was not going to be dissuaded from this decision.

We had other discussions about adoption. She felt that this was a way of neglecting her responsibilities. "I know that an adoptive parent may be better for the child and his/her future, but somehow I feel that I would be coping out and should accept my responsibility as a parent," she stated. She had the maturity to understand that any choice would have numerous repercussions.

Victoria decided to have the child. She was either too selfish or too conscientious to give her child up for adoption. I know that for her, it was the latter. I felt that she would make every effort to give the child the best home possible.

The next few months were agonizing, frustrating, and yet a bit exciting. Victoria continued to attend school and participate in parenting classes in preparation for a trying and uncertain future. She carried herself with a quiet dignity. She did not want any attention for the personal obstacles she was wrestling with. She seemed to do anything possible to avoid bringing attention to herself. Her grades remained solid, she continued supporting the school and its activities, and held down a part-time job as a manager of a fast-food restaurant.

I was amazed at how mature Victoria was in handling this complex problem. She would do absolutely nothing to bring attention to herself. Yet she would answer questions politely and, as a matter of fact, to avoid any ploy or baiting for attention.

After her son was born, Victoria even demonstrated a higher level of perceptivity and maturity. She met and exceeded all expectations as a parent. She hired a babysitter to help when she was working or at school. When the new semester began, she changed her schedule to allow more time for work and to be with her son. She downplayed the significance of what she was doing and saw herself as nothing special. She avoided all attention for her role yet maintained pride in her son without bringing attention to herself.

Her son was a true picture of a child who had a secure and well-adjusted home and self-image. He was intuitive, creative, gregarious, and intelligent. He was positive and openly interacted with adults. It was obvious that this child was loved and respected without being indulged. As a seventeen-year-old, Victoria demonstrated more maturity, responsibility, and human understanding that most adults do.

Today she maintains high goals for herself and her son. She is in her third year of college, and he is just entering the first grade. Although I would never wish the situation on any other person, I would never hesitate to refer to Victoria as a person who would offer wise and sound advice. I know that her style and approach to parenting would help any person learn to raise strong, compassionate, and self-reliant children. I hope that others have gained and learned from the responsibility and role model she exhibits.

Men, Not Boys

We are constantly looking for heroes. The media scrutinizes the background and projected image of an individual in hopes of constructing or finding a legend. Much of the time, the group that is instrumental in a great accomplishment, goes unnoticed because we look to attach a certain person to an event or niche in history. It seems that a group has little to offer in terms of colorful character or personality.

Most of the time, it is an individual, who seems to entrench themselves in the memory of observers. Every once in a while, an outstanding act offered by a group is attached to no particular person, and the purity of the act remains associated with the whole group.

One such group was a team that had little varsity experience and was almost void of seniors. Small size, limited experience, and questionable leadership characterized the group. Yet this team established itself as unique and special in terms of its response to adversity and overcoming obstacles.

We met the season head-on with high hopes, youthful enthusiasm, and a bundle of energy. The day before our opening game, a huge wall of adversity was placed in front of this team. Already shorthanded because two starters had missed a practice and were unable to play in the game, we were dealt another blow when two other starters were injured and unable to play the entire season. The severe shoulder dislocation and torn anterior cruciate ligament made the overall outlook seem a bit bleak. Injuries grew to the point that it almost seemed to be an epidemic. I can recall at least four different nights of waiting in the hospital to hear about the extent of injuries. I began to challenge myself and the organization of practices in hopes of finding an answer to that much too complex question. I arrived at no plausible solution and found myself hesitant even to initiate contact drills in practice.

However, the players on the team continued to upgrade their level of performance. They began playing highly favored opponents with determination and superior execution. Even though players had to make changes and the lineups for the games were never the same, they continued to raise their level of performance. All members of the team mixed the execution with an unselfish attitude.

We were beginning our final week of practice. If possible, the troops had an even higher level of enthusiasm. Now I could attribute this to the fact that a nightmare season was winding down and the pain was going to end or a genuine love for the team and the game itself. We were going to face an undefeated team in the last game of the season. Being 1-7, we obviously posed little threat to our opponents. Yet there seemed to be something special about the play and the hearts of these young men.

We came to our last practice of the season. When the team was called up at the completion of practice, they expressed a genuine desire to continue until we were satisfied that all bases were covered for the game the next day. I expressed that it was probably too dark to hold practice any longer. But the team pleaded for another half-hour. I obliged, and we completed the practice in an additional thirty-five minutes of complete darkness.

I felt confident that we would give the fans on both sides of the field a good show. As we walked on the field on that cold, wet, and foggy night, I could tell that the attitude was positive and upbeat. Their focus, fortitude, and ability to respond under adverse situations were even superseded by their concentration on this evening. Their eyes were riveted straight ahead, faces were sullen, and voices were muted. It was obvious that these young men were planning to upset the league champs. The first quarter was a hard-fought battle between the twenty-five-yard lines. Then with six minutes left in the second quarter, our opponents broke through with a thirty-yard touchdown pass. Two minutes later, a turnover resulted in another score. Despite being behind 13-0, our team remained focused and determined. On our own forty-three-yard line with fifteen seconds left in the half, we took our last time out with a fourth and six situation. We successfully called a hook and ladder play and scored as the horn sounded ending the half.

With renewed hope, we charged onto the field for the start of the second half. Four consecutive illegal plays brought me to the point of out-of-control anger. My constant challenging of the referee forced him to initiate my exit from the field. For the only time in my coaching career I was unable to fulfill my duties as a coach. As I watched us crumble in the second half from the outside of the field, I felt frustration, guilt, and yet admiration for these young men who were trying to keep the boat afloat without a rudder.

They fought gamely and maintained a much higher level of poise than their coach had. They never quit, and they managed a pride touchdown to pull us to a 34-13 deficit. Yet I could feel nothing but pride and respect for their ability to stay unified and poised. The pupils had become the teacher and the teacher the student. After pulling themselves aboard the bus, it was evident these undersized and inexperienced young warriors were open to any positive words offered. All I could offer was an apology and express my admiration for their character and maturity.

The bus ride home was strangely quiet. It was evident that these players did not want to end the season in this manner. Few outsiders can understand that these players were most upset about the season ending. They truly enjoyed the challenge and the game itself. Almost every player later expressed emptiness in their day and a true desire to continue the season. I think that all of us felt that our journey was not yet complete.

Upon arriving at the school, the coaches expressed a feeling of pride and appreciation. We then quietly filed off the bus. As usual, the coaches stayed behind with the manager to check the bus for personal items left and equipment. We then quietly made our way up the long and unlit driveway to the locker room. The assistant coaches either went into the office or helped the managers put the gear away. I went to the team room to check on the members of the team. When I opened the door, the lights were off and the room was empty. I searched the other team rooms and questioned the coaches to no avail. When we walked outside, we heard some commotion coming from the main field.

We could see shadows moving in the cold night on the playing surface. What we viewed and heard was what team and sacrifice are all about. After completing an injury-riddled season of 1-8, this team was running wind sprints and chanting our pride yells on a dark and wet field at 11:00 PM after the season was completed. After thirty minutes of hard running, they walked quietly, in single file, up the ramp and into the locker room. We said nothing. This was their statement of pride and heart. It was their private moment. Not one player said a word. Finally the last player paused as he walked by and whispered, "This is our statement of commitment for next year. A season like this will never happen again." As coaches, we knew that these young men had the internal fortitude and tenacity to make the predicted statement true. They had used a season of heartbreak yet united effort as a springboard. And more amazingly they went far beyond anybody's wildest expectations.

JODY OF ARC

Jody was a gifted athlete. Although not fast, she had superior court sense, excellent timing, and great hand-eye coordination. She would diligently strive to perfect moves and other skills. That may have been as much of a detriment as well as a blessing for Jody.

Jody demanded purity, honesty, and trustworthiness from herself. She expected this in others. She came from a loving, well-educated, and economically affluent family. It would be easy for such parents to spoil and indulge their children. It also would be easy to ignore or only relate on a surface level with their children. While Jody's parents held high expectations for her, they were primarily concerned about self-respect and human dignity. They instilled these fine virtues in Jody, maybe to a fault.

Jody set high goals for herself and friends or teammates. She understood shortcomings and failure in others but had a tendency not to tolerate these in herself. Her leaning to perfectionism made her a teacher and a coach's dream. Yet these traits may be a nightmare or curse to her.

One evening, I received a phone call from Jody's parents. They were emotional, confused, and frustrated. She had made a second attempt to take her own life. She may be one of the few people I categorize as being too good for society. I believe that she could readily identify with the personal pain and frustrations of others. These insights and high personal expectations caused anxiety when she was unable to offer perfect solutions. She demanded so much from herself that it became impossible for her to give perfect solutions to her own, as well as others' problems. This resulted in a hopeless state of futility.

Her parents were so concerned about her that selfish pride and social status did not enter their mind. They only cared about the welfare of their daughter. I truly marvel at parents who are so concerned about their child that they are not afraid to put their own ego or reputation on the back burner. They truly care only about the welfare of their child.

Jody's parents searched for solutions from many different sources. They had contacted counselors, the church, and various agencies. They also had asked me to spend time talking with her. Finally, her parents and I persuaded her to get help for this problem.

Jody was in a hospital for over a week where she received counseling. She returned to school three days after being released from the hospital. I was a bit apprehensive because the basketball practices were going to begin in three weeks. I did not want to burden her with further pressures. When we first spoke in the hallway, she seemed a bit uncertain and withdrawn. It was obvious that she felt a mixed bag of embarrassment and insecurity. But slowly, the stress and anxiety began to diminish.

Before the first practice began, we spoke a number of times about her goals and perceptions. It was our goal that she should attempt to create an understanding and tolerance for temporary failure. She need not lower her high standards of ethics, goals, and unselfish acts. She did need to gain an understanding of fallible behavior and actions. Through an examination of herself and an introspective look at society, Jody was able to sort out her feelings of inadequacy.

For the next two years, Jody grew stronger as a person. She maintained her high ideals and ethics without burying herself in societal failure. She became one of the top scholar athletes in the school. She would lead the younger athletes through and by example. She worked very hard to improve her skills and help lead the team to a pair of titles. But moreover, she learned the true intrinsic joy of playing the game. Basketball had become both rewarding and fun.

Jody received a full athletic scholarship to a top, prestigious Division I university. Midway through her freshman year she had become a full-time starter. And as a sophomore, she was averaging thirteen points and nine rebounds a game. The team was showing great strides and becoming a formidable foe. They had climbed to the upper half of the division, and it looked as if they would begin fighting for a playoff spot. Since Jody was an instrumental part of this success, I felt that her year was turning out to be a player's dream.

During the winter break, Jody came to school to observe practice and visit with the old coach. I was shocked to see her. I thought her team would be practicing and playing games during the break. I asked her why they were not practicing over the winter break. "They are practicing, but I am not playing anymore," she said. I looked at her in disbelief. "I have terminated my scholarship and decided to not play," she added. I mouthed why, but obviously my face had already given the message. "The program is filled with double standards and corruption. Grades have been doctored and credits undeservedly given," she stated. "But, Jody, could you not have spoken with the coach or appealed to the athletic director? This is so much to give up," I replied. "I have spent many hours talking with the coaching staff, administrators, and anybody I could," she said. "Everybody tried to soft-soap me and brush it under the carpet. I could not allow this to go on and inadvertently be a part of this farce. I needed to stand up for what was right. I could not mouth ethics and standards and participate in something as dishonest as this," she countered.

I knew she was right. But few people can stand on principle when it costs them so much. The sacrifice she made gave me an unbelievable sense of pride and admiration. Jody will always be a person of high personal standards and ethics. She would not let the "superficiality" of winning interfere with what is right. She made a stand that was solidly founded on principle and integrity.

She financed her last two years in college and is now experiencing a successful career in the legal field. And, oh yes, she is playing basketball for the love of the game.

No Obstacle Too Large

After knocking on the door for a full two minutes, I began to wonder if I had the right apartment or there had been confusion about the time. Grant was very reliable, and I had never known him to miss a time or appointment. We had agreed on a certain time to pick up the papers his parents had filled out on financial aid. I thought that I heard people moving around in the apartment. Finally, the door opened just a crack. A shaky voice came from inside the door. "Who is there, and what do you want," it quivered. "This is Coach Mac, and I came to get Grant's financial aid papers," I answered to the dark slit in the door. The chain was slowly removed, and the door creaked open.

"Come on in, Coach," the voice from the dark said. It was Grant's father. I hope I did not show the shock as I entered and gazed around the room. The dim lighting did not hide the yellow and crinkled newspapers spread around to serve as a makeshift carpet. Three old mattresses lay in lumpy heaps in various corners of the room. The peeled paint on the walls was partially hidden by the gray shadows and dingy lighting. The pot and booze odors were only masked partially by the unkempt and dirty dog. The smell gagged me, and I hoped this meeting would quickly end. I could not help but ask myself how it would be possible for a person to study or complete assignments under such conditions.

The father was in noticeable discomfort. His pain was partially masked by the use of various drugs. I knew that both parents were severely addicted to drugs. On numerous occasions, one or the other parent had been rushed to emergency because of drug overdose. Infections from dirty needles also were threats on lives of one or both parents. He finally was able to explain that Grant had been called to work because of an emergency. Apparently, he had not called because they did not have a phone. Before I left, I quickly jotted down a message for the father to give to Grant. I knew that the chance of him receiving the message was small, but at least I had tried to cover this base. As I made my way to the door, I briefly stumbled over one of the mattresses. As I looked down I could see urine spots dotting the various newspapers used as a carpet. I assumed or hoped that the dog made them.

As I walked out the door, I was relieved to get a brief smell of fresher air. Unfortunately, it quickly was engulfed by the smell of rotting garbage that had been strung about in front of the apartments. As I weaved my way in and out of cars, abandoned junk and children, I could not help but question the future of all of these young people. I wondered about how much untapped potential was going to waste.

Grant had always demonstrated tremendous strength and internal fortitude. As a sophomore he had sustained a serious knee injury. He had a torn anterior cruciate ligament, as well as damage to cartilage and lateral ligaments. The doctor said he virtually had to lay the knee out in three strips or segments. The tedious operation lasted for over four hours. After coming out of the operation, Grant was depressed and discouraged. He was worried about getting behind in school, his job and how to pay his medical bill.

Most of the bill was taken care of by the state, but the bills coming from the rehab program were his responsibility. He was not certain whether or not he wanted to play again. While giving him words of encouragement, I was careful not to put too much pressure on him to play the following season. I did not want him to play because of guilt or a feeling of responsibility to the coaches or the program.

But this was a full-throttle man. He never gave less than 100 percent in practice or games. This young man would always give full effort on every drill, conditioner, and play. This toughness carried over to the rehabilitation program. He put himself through exhausting pain and effort. He would do extra exercises to help facilitate the healing process. The doctors had told him that with hard work, he could return to work without crutches by spring and to full activity by next fall. We were not surprised to see him attack this in full force. By spring he was lifting weights and preparing for the track season. He also was working thirty hours a week and maintaining a 3.75 GPA. The doctor told me that he had never witnessed a person fight through pain so hard to improve his flexibility and strength in such a short time. By August he was ready for football camp.

That season and the following he performed at an all-star level on both sides of the ball. The only problem we ever had was to hold the reins and keep him from practicing too hard. In three years of varsity football, he never loafed on a single drill. Incredible! During his senior year, he was by far and away the most dominating player in the league. He was unanimous choice All-League running back and linebacker.

I felt strongly that this multitalented athlete had a tremendous future at the next level and beyond. He could tackle, run, and throw. He was one of the best kickers I have seen at the high school or college level. He may well be the best-blocking back I have coached or witnessed. He was determined, positive, and unselfish. He would always place the well-being of the team first. He was an excellent student who had the discipline, intelligence, and determination to excel at the college level. But the visions I had foreseen never came to fruition.

I am not sure what were the main factors that kept him from taking advantage of a full college scholarship, but I suspect it had to do with his feeling of responsibility to his family. His parents experienced so much in terms of personal and health problems that they never were able to give much time or support to Grant. Oh, they used a few familiar adjectives such as good and smart son. But the statements seemed so empty and lacked any depth of feeling or understanding. Their extreme chemical dependence was primarily instrumental in leading to indifference toward the children, sickness, unemployment, and poor living conditions. It is an all-too-common tragedy. They had missed out on so much, and it would never be recovered.

Even though his parents had never seen him participate in sports, attended school conferences or award ceremonies, he had a strong love and emotional tie. With his parents experiencing ill health, he had become the strength or rock of the family. It was ironic that even though they had never supported him, he was there to support them. What a man of character and strength!

Today Grant is very successful in a number of ways. He is married, has purchased a home, is a highly paid manager of a company, and has two children. Grant truly has overcome overwhelming odds to reach for the stars. I now realized that I should not "box up" or restrict the essence or meaning of success. Grant is truly a hero in so many ways. And one thing that I am sure of is that Grant will be there for his children.

SHE THOUGHT SHE COULD

I have always felt that it does not necessarily require a lot of character to be positive in competitive athletics when everything is going your way. I suppose that some people would claim that a statement of this nature is only a bandage for a loser. However, for an extremely talented and gifted individual, their internal strength and fortitude may never be challenged. Hopefully, as the person raises their level of competition, there is a much-greater risk of failure or adversity. But when they are not gifted, the challenge may be just too tough for the average person to deal with. Consequently, they become satisfied or accept poor performance and eventually quit with a bitter attitude.

It takes a person of superior character to continue to grow despite failure and poor performance in the eyes of society. To never give up or become complacent about your achievement may well be the ultimate challenge.

Jeannie had never been involved in any athletic endeavor. We had discussed, on a few occasions, about some sort of activity she could find a measure of success through. Eventually, by the time spring rolled around, she accepted the challenge to go out for track. "You know that I have no talent or knowledge about sports," she exclaimed. "But I am going to give this a try so you will quit bugging me," she added. After the first practice, I could tell that she was even slower, weaker, and less coordinated than I had imagined. Obviously, the challenge would be to have her stick it out for the entire season. What made the matter even more complex, Jeannie was intuitive and perceptive. Consequently, she was aware of her inadequacy. She also was competitive and very determined. This would give a push and a desire to succeed. Unfortunately, her desire to compete and win did not correlate or fit well with little talent, strength, and experience.

She spent the first two weeks experimenting with each event in hopes of finding a niche. She soon discovered that she was equally inept in each event. During challenge week, she had to limit her choice to four events. As one may expect, she finished last in all four events. Despite her frustration, she tried in vain to keep an upbeat facade. She had repeatedly heard the message of how the most important goal can only be achieved from within. And I am sure she knew that boundaries are only limited to your own shortsightedness. Yet she doubted herself and her ego was being challenged.

Track is a sport where competition with oneself is practical and beneficial. However, since society primarily measures success in terms of extrinsic rewards, that idealistic goal seemed to lose its power for Jeannie. She had a forced smile on her face when I came to talk to her about the events she would be scheduled to perform. Fortunately, the dreaded distance events had no restrictions in terms of participation. I also felt that she would be able to identify improvement quickly and consistently in these events. When I told her that I thought these would be her best events, she appeared relieved to know that she had some ownership on the team.

Girls' track was relatively new, and there were only two levels. Many schools struggled just to fill out a varsity lineup. We did not have this problem. We had to find events where we could have each person participate. The two-mile and mile were the only events where all participants ran together. The jerseys or numbers they wore identified the levels. This could work for or against Jeannie. She could get lost in the group or be humiliated in a massive defeat.

With the first meet just around the corner, it was easy to detect her apprehension and anxiety. She took out her frustration by working extra-hard in hopes of closing the gap between her and the other girls. Finally, the day of the first meet arrived. Even though Jeannie remained focused on school all day, every once in a while she would mentally drift. I am sure that very few people would be able to detect the anxiety she was feeling. She did an excellent job of maintaining poise, but her stomach must have been churning.

As the first event began, Jeannie was there to cheer and encourage her teammates. I am sure it must have seemed like an eternity before her first event began. Finally the last call for the mile was made. As they lined up, I could see Jeannie looking across the line in hopes of assurance from her teammates. Two girls looked back, smiled, and nodded in a show of support.

There were over fifteen girls in the event. The gun fired, and the pack of young athletes began a grueling race. Within the first two hundred yards, Jeannie was already sixty yards behind the leaders. Her slow, loping strides seemed to be weighed down by her feet of stone. By the end of the first lap, she trailed the entire field by more than one hundred yards. And by the time she completed her second turn around the track, she had been lapped by the first two runners. Before she completed the third lap, the entire field had already crossed the finish line. As her feet slapped loudly on the asphalt track surface, Jeannie approached the final one hundred yards. Many of the members of both teams applauded her. Even though this was heartwarming, I could not help but wonder about how much of the applause was given out of respect and how much because of condescending pity. Her face was flushed, and she struggled to get her breath. She looked at me with this blank stare. I wondered what was going through her mind. I could not tell if she was relieved, disappointed, or embarrassed. But one thing I was certain of was that she had quickly become indoctrinated into the world of athletic competition.

During the two mile, she was lapped either two or three times by the entire competition. I knew that the humiliation would be tough for her to fight. But she did not waiver or falter. She continued to work hard to reach her personal goals. She consistently would knock one to three seconds off her time. By the end of the season, she had raced a few times without being lapped by the entire field in the mile.

The next school year, Jeannie decided to go out for cross-country. Again, she finished last in every meet. But she stuck with the team and completed the season. During her sophomore season in track, she demonstrated renewed hope. She continued to work hard despite repeated failures. By the time the next to the last meet rolled around, she still had finished last in both events despite improving her times. Yet her hard work finally paid a dividend. In the two mile, she sprinted the final two hundred yards to pass a young girl from the other school. You would think that she had won the state championship. She had tears in her eyes as many of the team approached her with enthusiasm and congratulations. In the final meet she again defeated another opponent. After two years of running, she was finally over a big hurdle.

Things really began to look up. As a junior, she finished consistently in the middle of the pack. She even finished third in one meet. She finished thirteenth in the city meet.

Unfortunately, eight of the young ladies who had beaten her were underclassmen. Even though she had come so far, she now focused on new goals.

As a senior, she finished eighth in the city cross-country meet. This inspired her to train all winter for her final season. All of the adversity, humiliation, and hard work began to pay big dividends. She began her senior season with high hopes. She actually finished first in three of the meets and consistently won points for the team. "Wouldn't it be a dream if I could finish in the top three in districts and go to state," she said to me. "But you know, Coach, all of this work and pain is valuable by itself. The winning is just the cream on top," she added. This young lady had climbed an unbelievable mountain and was able to see the true beauty at the end. She loved the sport, the inner strength it brought out in her, and her improved self-image. I guess it was not that important whether or not she won. What was important was that she had met challenges with dogged determination and heart. She had fought a battle few of us will ever understand. She was already a champion. I can only imagine the euphoria she must have felt. Oh, and for the extrinsically minded people, she did win the two-mile event at districts and went to state. But more importantly, she won the respect and admiration of all associated with her, including herself. I came across Jeannie at a local mall about fifteen years later. She proudly introduced me to her three children. It seemed that she relished in tackling the tough role of parenting, with the same enthusiasm, determination, and sparkle in her eyes she had demonstrated as an athlete. Her children reflected her positive attitude and zest for life. It certainly was a testimony of the parallels one can note between athletics and other avenues of life.

I Love You Too Much to Hurt

At 4:30 PM, during preseason practice in late November, I heard this loud commotion coming from the halls. I "flung" open the gym door to see bodies crashing and garbage cans flying. There were three girls scratching and clawing each other like alley cats. I grabbed one and yelled at the other two to knock it off.

I wanted to know why these three "ladies" were fighting each other as if there was no tomorrow. What even put a brighter shine on this wonderful event was that they were all members of the freshmen basketball team. Apparently, two sisters were angry with their best friend. With confidence and a sense of pride, one sister exclaimed, "Don't worry, Coach, we always fight like this. Sometimes, Allisha teams with one of us against the other." Internally I was amused but had to demonstrate disgust and disappointment. "Well, in this program, you work together as a team and eliminate your petty differences and feuds," I replied. Stoically they nodded. "Do you understand? I do not want to see this type of behavior again," I forcefully stated. But it was evident that the message had no real internal impact.

It was obvious that these young ladies were skilled at maneuvering their feisty characteristics to fit in or appease the powers that be.

Although we had no further instances that were of a physical nature, we had to continue working eliminating the verbal attacks directed at each other. Most of the time one or both of the sisters would make a verbal attack or "cheap shot" at Allisha. However, on the court it was a different story. Once the game began, it was fun to watch these little hornets play basketball together. They would fly all over the place, harassing and stealing the ball from more fundamental and gentler opponents. These mighty mites could intimidate almost all opposition. Unfortunately, all three were usually sitting on the bench with five fouls before the game was over. Toning down and teaching these athletes to play under control was extremely difficult. I must add that my assistant coach may have lost some hair but did a very commendable job of controlling and not inhibiting these little "buzz-saws."

What we did note was there was so much beneath the tough exterior that Allisha exhibited to others. It was almost like she needed the facade to protect a fragile ego. She seemed to be a person who had a sense of order, justice, and feeling for others. It was obvious that she had experienced turmoil and instability in her childhood. But there seemed to be so much depth and feeling that was always looking for ways to break out. During the summer before her sophomore year, Allisha played on the varsity basketball team. It was gratifying to watch her help provide the team with emotional and physical inspiration.

However, because of problems at school and in the classroom, the sisters were unable to compete. Although the sisters and Allisha took different avenues of interest, they remained close friends.

Allisha continued to grow as a student-athlete and became a leader on the court and in the classroom. On one occasion during class, we had been discussing social relationships and true friendship. We were attempting to identify true and honest concern for people without selfish reference. One student raised a concern. Would a true friend sacrifice reputation, subject him or her to social ridicule, and even risk a personal relationship for the well-being of somebody they cared for? If you knew a friend was involved in dangerous activities, would you do anything to keep them from being hurt? Would you even tell their parents or the authorities if you really cared about their well-being? We concluded that, even though admirable, few of us would be strong enough to sacrifice ourselves socially and emotionally for others.

A week later, Allisha came to me after class. She was deeply concerned about the sisters. She said that she had been making a sincere effort to evaluate her commitment to her friends. It seems that both had been using cocaine and were dabbling in more serious drugs. She said that she had confronted them on numerous occasions. They would brush off the confrontation or express anger toward Allisha. They would give the all-too-often phrase, "it is none of your business." Allisha countered by saying that she would take any steps necessary to keep them from destroying their lives. She was at her wit's end about possible solutions. It seemed that everything she tried had no effect. Allisha and I agreed that if she were going to tell their parents, she would have to warn the sisters first.

The next time they were together, Allisha told them if they did not stop using drugs, she would tell their parents. They tried to con her by assuring her that they were stopping. She called their bluff. A physical confrontation followed. As Allisha walked away from their house, she could hear threats and bleeps following her. But she remained strong in her intentions, her word, and herself. Later that week, she met with their parents and revealed the shocking news. The parents immediately confronted the sisters. After denial, anger, and contradictions, the parents concluded that Allisha was telling the truth. The parents made some drastic attempts to curb their daughters' self-destructive activities. Privileges and social relationships were eliminated or controlled. Strict rules were imposed, and both girls were referred to counseling.

The next turn of events could almost be expected. The girls would not speak with Allisha. Their friends at school ignored or threw verbal shots when she would walk down the halls. She was threatened and assaulted. Since the search for social acceptance and security is a primary concern for teenagers, the weeks that followed must have been excruciatingly painful for Allisha. "This has been a very tough time for me, Coach. I am lonely at times. Although I do feel I am at peace with my decision and I know that was right and was done for their best interest, the social ridicule and rejection hurts," she said. As so oftentimes happens, doing the positive thing had only brought about negative responses. A just and moral person suffered injustice from ignorant and shortsighted people. But Allisha never gave up on trying to bridge the gap between her and the sisters. She tried to communicate by letter or visitation with the sisters, but they refused to respond. Eventually, they withdrew from school and completely pulled away. Yet I do not believe that Allisha ever quit caring for their well-being.

It was two years before the sisters approached Allisha. Finally one of the sisters visited her at her home. Through tearful eyes and with a shaky voice, she said, "Allisha, you were the only friend who really cared about us. I know now that what you did may have saved our lives. Even though my sister is having a harder time of shaking the drugs, she is also thankful for what you did," she said. Sometimes brave and unselfish acts receive the best of belated rewards. Allisha and the sisters have since rekindled and maintained a strong and loving friendship. How lucky they were to have a true friend like Allisha.

Another demonstration of unselfish maturity was discovered through class discussions. One of our sociology units dealt with the family, marriage, and parenting. Needless to say, we had numerous discussions that were revealing and emotional. On one occasion we were talking about parent-child relationships. Many students had expressed numerous examples of parental strengths and weaknesses. Allisha was unusually quiet but showed a keen interest in each example. After class, she related an amazing story. "You may already know that my parents have had a very difficult life. My mom has tried to support all six of us emotionally. However, my dad has done very little for us as a father. He only talks with us when he is angry. His only emotion revolves around punishment. He is abusive to all of the children. Although he does not hit us as much as he used to, his emotional abuse has increased. It is so hard to respect my father." We talked a bit about her perspective and discussed a few techniques that could help her cope with a heavy situation.

About a week later, she came to me after class and relayed a remarkable series of events. "Last night my father was 'mean drunk.' He was yelling swear words at all of us. Suddenly he started coming toward me with his fist clinched. I was scared and uncertain about what to do," she said. Suddenly she rushed toward and threw her arms around him. "I told him that I loved him too much to allow him to hit me again. I wanted to show my love and respect for him," she relayed. "I know that he has reason for his actions. I know they are wrong, but I believe that he is doing the best that he can to control himself," she said with tears flowing down her face.

I was speechless to say the least. Here was this brave and courageous young lady of seventeen years playing the role of a most understanding and mature adult. Despite the emotional pain, Allisha had gained a clear perspective of a very complex problem. She had discovered reason and logic in what most people would feel to be an intolerable situation. She was able to look past the weak and what I perceived to be inexcusable actions of her father. Through perception and patience, she had in effect become the parent.

Her father never hit Allisha again. I guess he knew that this young lady was very unique. Their relationship grew after that point. The family still struggled. However, they now had a pillar of strength to build on. The father and mother had discovered their ray of hope. She had become the glue and foundation of a weak and dysfunctional family.

Today Allisha is raising two sons and coaching high school basketball. Her children and players demonstrate a true unselfish, respectful, and dignified attitude. I wonder where they discovered those traits.

CHAPTER REVIEW

1. I Can See the Joy through Your Eyes
   A. Change reveals the unselfish and altruistic heart
   B. Reciprocation results in unexplained miracle

2. There Is Tough and There Is Sally
   A. Expectations and self imposed standards inspire others
   B. Patronizing or courtesy

3. Does Your View Put Limits on Me
   A. Personal adversity breaks guarded chains
   B. You said—I can't

4. It Is My Fault
   A. Real strength is measured by constructive self criticism
   B. Principle vs. desired fame

5. Diplomacy Opened by Integrity
   A. Can honesty and integrity overcome extrinsic goals
   B. Respect overcomes human differences and ideas

6. So I Can't or Won't You Say
   A.Ignorance and prejudice are roadblocks to growth or change
   B.Walk the talk because pure talk is cheap

7. Don't Undersell Me, I Will Finish
   A.Tough expectations may be the highest of compliments
   B.Challenged people need not be sold short

8. It's Time to Grow Up and Take Care of Your House
   A.Doing the right thing is tougher and requires inner confidence
   B.To respect and include all requires confidence

9. Say There Is More—or Not
   A.Adversity brings unification
   B.True success measured in depth

10. Are You Laughing Now?
    A.Personal talent and success can bring apprehension and jealousy in others
    B.Talent is the flare while effort is the foundation

11. Don't Step on My Lip
    A.A means to motivation is not predictable
    B.Self Image relates to imposed goals

12. Maybe Quality Does Count
    A.Quality may require time and still be overlooked
    B.I understand—I just can't

13. I Have another Side
    A. Your labels can help bring about your stereotype
    B. Buffoonery can wear the cloak of confidence

14. No Limits from Social Structure
    A. I must earn; not be given
    B. Striving for excellence in the self cancels hypocrisy

15. You Only Know Part of Me
    A. I fooled everyone but myself
    B. Leadership needs to be demonstrated beyond the norm

16. Even Good Leaders May Win
    A. Leadership acknowledged for action rather than show
    B. Do we sacrifice principles for security and status?

17. The Power to Overcome the Odds
    A. Avoid shame of self and your people
    B. I chose the game and accept the rules

18. Leadership Not Restricted to Show
    A. Does talent correlate with respect or leadership?
    B. My joy is through your success

19. Are You Still Mocking Me from Behind?
    A. I am not weird-just diverse
    B. Your Anchor and stereotypes need not force limits on me

20. What You See Is Not Who I Am
    A. What you see is not who I am
    B. I have nothing to lose except pride

21. Ruggedly Sweet and Straight
    A. Principal always takes precedence
    B. Caring can be expressed in so many different ways

22. Responsibility Need Not Be Boastful
    A. Love is quiet unassuming and comes privately
    B. Extra work does not mean failure

23. Men Not Boys
    A. Love the Game, not the fame
    B. Never too early to start working on goals

24. Jody of Arc
    A. Perfection challenges a feeling of inadequacy
    B. Honesty can hurt in so many ways but . . .

25. No Obstacle Too Large
    A. My success may be outside of your vision
    B. Giving may not be justified, reciprocated but it is enough in itself

26. She Thought She Could
    A. I cannot find a niche
    B. Losing can create apathy, acceptance and to most futility

27. I Love You Too Much to Hurt
   A. Is it possible that pain and ridicule creates love and respect
   B. Success seems to be impossible to attain against such odds

Printed in the United States
125946LV00003B/245/P

9 781436 319232